Teacher's Guide

FOR

Ellen J. Rank

Behrman House Publishers
www.behrmanhouse.com

Book and Cover Design: Joe Buchwald Gelles
Project Editor: Terry S. Kaye
Art by Ron Zalme

Springfield, New Jersey 07081
www.behrmanhouse.com
ISBN-10: 0-87441-783-X
ISBN-13: 978-0-87441-783-8
Manufactured in the United States of America

Contents

Introduction

Hebrew, the language of our people, is both ancient and modern. Modern Hebrew, which has its roots in biblical and siddur Hebrew, is a vibrant language that is constantly adapting to life in Israel today. It is spoken in the streets, houses, and malls, and in the movie theaters, coffee shops, and supermarkets of Israel.

Let's Talk! Modern Hebrew for Teens is an upbeat and engaging text that will make teaching modern conversational Hebrew a delight. As your students learn to speak Hebrew, they will gain a greater understanding of the daily life and culture of Israel today. Their connection to Israel and the language of the Jewish people will deepen as their knowledge and fluency in Hebrew grow.

Let's Talk! will introduce your students to Hebrew through humorous dialogues, attractive illustrations, and age-appropriate exercises. From the airport in New York to floating in the Dead Sea, buying gifts in the *shuk* in Be'er-Sheva, working on a kibbutz, swimming in Eilat, and riding a camel in the desert, your students will experience the travel adventures of four young people — Maya, a New Yorker who is traveling with her parents, Ben from Mexico, Dinah, a Toronto native, and Daniel, who hails from Los Angeles.

Let's Talk! will help your students:

- Increase fluency in reading Hebrew.
- Gain confidence in speaking Hebrew.
- Develop skills in Hebrew composition.
- Become familiar with cities and places in Israel.
- Deepen their understanding of Israeli culture.

Wishing you and your students נְסִיעָה טוֹבָה (a good trip) as you journey through ***Let's Talk!***

Method and Structure of *Let's Talk!*

Let's Talk! is designed to introduce bar and bat mitzvah-age students to modern Hebrew. Its goal is to entertain while educating. A new door will open for students as they acquire vocabulary, learn to build Hebrew sentences, and begin to converse in Hebrew.

Let's Talk! consists of fifteen chapters, each beginning with a two-page, easy-to-read dialogue followed by four pages of reinforcing activities. Through the dialogues students will become familiar with four young travelers who meet en route to Israel. Students will learn about places in Israel and Israeli culture as they travel to:

A kibbutz	Tel Aviv	The Dead Sea
Haifa	The Negev desert	Masada
Jerusalem	Eilat	Be'er-Sheva

Each of the fifteen chapters contains the following recurring features:

- An all-Hebrew dialogue that immerses students in modern conversational Hebrew.
- A *milon* — מִלוֹן (dictionary) — that introduces and translates new vocabulary.
- Four pages of activities that reinforce vocabulary and grammar taught in the current as well as in previous chapters.
- A photograph of Israel that provides a visual teaching opportunity.

Recurring exercises, designed to reinforce both passive and active language acquisition, include:

Make the Connection Students connect words in one column to their matching words in a second column.

You're the Author Students choose words from a word bank to correctly complete a sentence.

Yes or No? Students answer questions based on the chapter's dialogue.

Perfect Fit Students choose a correct word to complete a sentence and then read the sentence aloud.

Picture Match Students connect a Hebrew word or phrase to a matching illustration.

Search and Circle Students circle the English meaning for Hebrew words.

Vocabulary and grammar acquisition is cumulative. The dialogues and activities include new words and word forms while they build on those that have been presented in earlier chapters. Each chapter is filled with delightful illustrations that bring the dialogues and activities to life.

Linguistic Approach in *Let's Talk!*

Learning to speak any new language is a challenge; learning to speak Hebrew is especially challenging for a native English speaker. Hebrew grammar is not at all like English grammar. Most Hebrew and English words have entirely different origins, and the written symbols and sounds are different. Students are unlikely to hear Hebrew spoken outside of the religious school. In short, Hebrew is a totally foreign language!

Let's Talk! introduces students to vocabulary, phrases, and grammatical structures that are used in everyday conversations through entertaining dialogues set in Israel. *Let's Talk!* eases students into actively speaking Hebrew in the following ways:

- Vocabulary has been carefully selected. Many of the words are related to Israel, allowing students to both *learn* about and *speak* about Israel. The choice of vocabulary also helps strengthen a connection to Israel and a desire to visit the land, and a motivation to speak Hebrew. Imagine the thrill of knowing that one could walk into a restaurant and order a falafel and a drink, all in Hebrew!
- Numerous cognates, such as קוֹלָה and טֶלֶפוֹן, appear in the dialogues. These words, which expand the students' vocabulary banks, are easy to learn and give students a sense of mastery.
- Students learn to recognize masculine and feminine forms from suffixes, for example, ָה or ת, for feminine, and they learn to recognize the plural from the suffixes ִים and וֹת.
- The verb forms are presented in the present tense in order to minimize complex and irregular conjugations and to create a sense of currency.
- Verbs are combined with infinitives, enabling students to develop more complicated sentences and to better express personal feelings.
- Only first and second person pronouns (I, we, and you) appear in *Let's Talk!* This underscores the emphasis on active conversation.

Let's Talk! is designed to make the acquisition of Hebrew reading, comprehension, and speaking skills a joy for your students — and to inspire and encourage them to learn more.

Time Management

Each of the fifteen chapters in *Let's Talk!* consists of six pages. If your school meets for thirty weeks, you should plan to study a new chapter approximately every two weeks. Keep in mind that while chapters have a consistent number of pages, there is a wide variation in the length of the dialogue and the number of vocabulary words presented in each chapter. For ideas on how to pace the teaching of vocabulary words, refer to "The Milon" on page 10.

Divide each class session into at least four distinct components:

1. An opening activity to review previous material or to set up the current session
2. Introduction of new material
3. Reinforcement of new material
4. A closing activity to summarize and reinforce the lesson's content

Remember that *Let's Talk!* emphasizes spoken Hebrew. Design your lessons so that your students have fun and enjoy learning to converse in Hebrew. While your lessons will include reading and writing Hebrew, be sure to emphasize conversation and making Hebrew a living, interactive language. Create a lesson plan in advance of every class session to manage your time so that you meet your goals.

What's in This Teaching Guide

This teaching guide is divided into three sections:

1. TEACHING STRATEGIES

This section offers ideas for games, conversation exercises, presentation of dialogues and new vocabulary, implementing and reviewing activities, and collaborative learning experiences that can be used throughout *Let's Talk!* A checklist for creating a classroom conducive to Hebrew learning is included in this section, as are suggestions for using the recurring features.

2. ENRICHMENT IDEAS FOR CHAPTERS

Here you will find activities, games, hands-on projects, and conversation starters specific to each chapter. Feel free to choose activities that best suit your teaching style as well as the interests and educational needs of your students. These icons will help you easily use the materials presented:

Set inductions to introduce the dialogues

Suggestions for Hebrew conversation in your classroom

Activities involving art, music, or food

Games and activities to reinforce vocabulary and grammar

Ideas for using the photographs and illustrations

3. ANSWERS TO ACTIVITIES

The four activity pages in each of the fifteen chapters of *Let's Talk!* are reproduced, with the answers written in.

Teaching Strategies

This section provides suggestions and techniques for teaching *Let's Talk!* and its recurring features most effectively. You may wish to refer back to this section as you plan your lessons for each chapter.

Creating a Hebrew Environment

If your students find pleasure and meaning in Hebrew, they will more likely absorb and retain their knowledge of Hebrew throughout their lives. Hebrew posters and music, as well as the use of Hebrew in everyday classroom routines, will help make the language real and accessible. To create a Hebrew environment in your classroom:

- Label classroom items with their Hebrew names.
- Hang an Israeli flag and a map of Israel in your classroom.
- Hang an *alef bet* chart, word cards, and attractive Hebrew posters on the walls.
- Display images and products of Israel, including Hebrew newspapers and magazines, or food products with Hebrew labels.
- Call on students using their Hebrew names. This will not only help your students feel more comfortable with spoken Hebrew, but will also reinforce a sense of Jewish identity and belonging.
- Take attendance and ask other routine questions in Hebrew.
- Encourage the students to answer in Hebrew, saying, for example, אֲנִי פֹּה (I am here).
- Play Hebrew music at the beginning of class as students are arriving, during class when students are working on projects, and at the end of class as students are packing up to leave.
- Set the home page of your classroom computer to an Israeli web site. Use a scene from Israel as wallpaper for the computer.
- Have simple Hebrew books and Hebrew versions of familiar English children's books available for children who finish their work early.
- Have two clocks in the classroom — one set to local time and the other set to Israeli time.

Learning Styles

Students learn in a variety of ways. You can enrich the classroom experience for all your students by acknowledging this diversity and providing meaningful experiences for each type of learner. Here are a few ways to create effective learning opportunities for:

1. ***Visual learners.*** Ask questions that require students to imagine themselves in or to interpret the chapters' photos or illustrations.
2. ***Auditory learners.*** Give your students plenty of opportunities to both hear and speak Hebrew. Encourage short conversations.
3. ***Kinesthetic ("learn by doing") learners.*** Have students role play the scenes depicted in the illustrations, draw objects on the board and name them, act out vocabulary words, or pantomime sentences from the dialogues.
4. ***Group learners.*** Create cooperative learning groups to develop activities. Stress individual accountability: Assign each student a clearly defined function within the group, such as reader, recorder, or presenter. Give each group the opportunity to present its work to the class.

Using the Recurring Features

Let's Talk! contains a number of features that appear in many of the chapters. These features provide students with opportunities to practice their Hebrew in the context of a familiar, repeating format. The following are some ways you may wish to use these recurring features. (Please note that ideas for using the chapters' photographs and illustrations may be found in the section "Enrichment Ideas for Chapters.")

The Milon

Every chapter contains a מִלּוֹן (dictionary) — a list of vocabulary words introduced in that chapter. Present the words to your class before they read the chapter dialogue. To do so, you can:

- Use a new word in a Hebrew sentence and have students guess its meaning.
- Say a new word as you act it out. Again, have students guess its meaning.
- Bring in objects or pictures of objects listed in the *milon*. Hold them up as you tell students the Hebrew words for these objects or pictures.
- Have students repeat the new word and then repeat a sentence that includes that word.
- Challenge students to use the new words in a sentence.
- Invent — or have your students invent — ways to remember the meaning of new words. For example, קַר (cold) sounds like "car," and one rides in a car when it is cold.
- Conduct easy oral quizzes by saying a Hebrew word and having volunteers translate it aloud into English. Increase the challenge by saying an English word and having students translate it into Hebrew.
- Have students read the *milon* in unison as a review.

***Hint for teaching a long* milon:**

Divide longer *milonim* into shorter lists. Your students will be happier and more successful when required to learn a maximum of seven words in a lesson. When teaching chapter 7, for example, you will see that there are nineteen words in the *milon*. While you will need to introduce — perhaps by having students read aloud — the entire *milon* before students hear the dialogue, you should focus on only the first seven words during the first lesson. Present those seven words as described above. Play a short game or conduct a short drill with just those seven words. During the reading of the dialogue, have students refer to the *milon* for the meaning of all new words.

During the second lesson, focus on the next six words, fully presenting each of those words, and then doing an activity or game that reviews those words along with the first seven. During the third lesson, present the remainder of the words and review all the words from the *milon*.

The Dialogue

Each chapter begins with a simple and often humorous dialogue among the travelers. Plan ahead to present these dialogues in varied and interesting ways. Since *Let's Talk!* emphasizes conversational Hebrew, your students should hear and speak all or parts of a dialogue before they read it. This will help auditory learners and will increase the class's fluency in speaking. At first, students can be less reliant on the written word and can focus instead on the skills needed for conversational Hebrew. They will have an opportunity to read the dialogues after they have heard and repeated them orally.

Keep the following suggestions in mind as you plan your lessons:

- *Capture your students' interest.* Use set inductions before beginning a new dialogue to stimulate your students' interest and to focus their attention. You will find suggestions for set inductions ("Introducing the Dialogue" has questions and discussions that set the mood for the dialogue) in the section "Enrichment Ideas for Chapters." Set inductions help students to relate personally to the dialogues. You might also ask your students to look at the *milon* and to guess, based on the *milon*, what will take place in the dialogue.

- *Be an actor.* As you present the dialogue, students' books should be closed. Direct students to look at you and listen as you read the new dialogue. You may choose to:
  - Include props, such as sunglasses for Daniel (Los Angeles), a maple leaf garment for Dina (Toronto), a sombrero for Ben (Mexico), and an "I love NY" sign for Maya (New York). Use a prop as you say each character's lines.
  - Change where you stand for each character, pretending that the characters are all speaking to one another.
  - Alter your voice for each character to reflect their personalities. Make the dialogue funny by speaking in a very low or very high voice.
  - Be dramatic; use hand and body motions to make the presentation more interesting and to aid student comprehension.
  - Draw an illustration on the board or hang a poster about Israel that is related to the dialogue.

- *Be a model.* For dialogue with short sentences, you should say one line at a time, and have students echo you. Repeat the line several times until students can say it easily and fluently.
  - To make the repetition entertaining change the tone of your voice and have students repeat the line in the same kind of voice.
  - Have students mimic your hand or body motions.
  - You may want to divide the class into groups, and have each group represent a specific character and echo the lines of its character. After presenting the dialogue once, assign each group to be a different character and repeat the dialogue.

- *Discuss the dialogue.* Ask students questions about the dialogue. Vary questions to be both simple, such as הַחֲבֵרִים רוֹצִים לִנְסוֹעַ לְאֵילַת? (Do the friends want to travel to Eilat?), and more complex, for example, מַה צָרִיךְ בְּאֵילַת? (What does one need in Eilat?). Applaud your students for answering questions with their books closed. If your students have difficulty answering the questions, allow them to refer to the book.

- *Have students present the dialogue.* Divide the class into groups, assigning each person in a group to be a particular character. Give the groups time to practice the dialogue. Encourage students to memorize their lines as this will help with fluency. Allow students to use props for the different characters. Ask for a group to present the dialogue. If you have several groups, you may want to stagger the presentations and have only one or two groups present a dialogue on a given day. Other groups can present the dialogue as the opening activity for subsequent lessons on that chapter.

Remember to vary your techniques to maintain interest!

Chapter Activities

Each chapter includes four pages of exercises designed to reinforce both passive and active use of the vocabulary and grammar presented in *Let's Talk!* Once students understand the dialogue, they are ready for the exercises.

1. ***Completing the activity.*** Call on a student to read aloud both the title of the activity and the instructions. To ensure that students understand the directions you may choose to:

   - Ask for a volunteer to do the first exercise as an example for the class.
   - Ask all students to do the first exercise independently and then review the answer together.
   - Refer students to an earlier page that has a similar activity.

   After all students understand the instructions, direct them to complete the activity individually, in pairs, or in groups.

2. ***Reviewing the activity.*** To check students' work you may choose to:

   - Invite a student to the front of the room to be the teacher. That student may then call on classmates to give the answers. You may want to write the answers on the board to help the visual learners.
   - Direct students to compare their answers with their neighbor's answers. If there are discrepancies, they should check with other classmates. Walk around the room, making sure students have the correct answers.
   - Call on different students to read their answers.

   It is essential that all students both check and correct their work. Simply marking an answer as incorrect will not help the student to learn. Make sure that your students are correcting all the exercises and that they understand the answer. Collect and review your students' textbooks at the end of a chapter for assessment.

3. ***Making accommodations.*** It is important to plan for the students who finish work quickly as well as for those who work slowly.

   The students who work quickly will need enrichment activities to maximize learning. You might, for example, challenge those students to:

   - memorize several lines of the chapter dialogue.
   - write a short story using new vocabulary words.
   - rewrite a dialogue changing sentences from masculine to feminine or vice versa.
   - create their own activities, games, or quizzes.

   Adjust the work load for slower workers. You may want to:

   - direct slower learners to complete only a portion of the exercise, such as four out of six items.
   - assign them shorter lines of dialogue to read aloud.
   - leave the assignment open-ended by telling them to complete as much as they can within a certain time.

   Above all, give lots of encouragement.

4. ***Building on the activities.*** Some types of activities recur in several chapters. The following ideas will help you build on these activities to add variety to your lessons.

   Most activities can be expanded to give your students greater exposure to the new vocabulary and grammar. Invite your students to think of new ways to present these activities. They will be delighted when you use their ideas as a class activity.

Search and Circle
Challenge students to say the Hebrew for the words that they have not circled.

Word Search Ask students to read a sentence from the dialogue that includes a word from the Word Search.

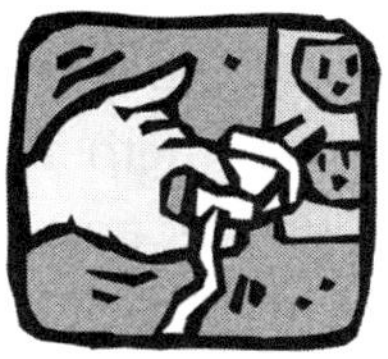

Make the Connection Direct students to cover all the English words and to say the English for each of the Hebrew words.

Perfect Fit Have students create sentences that include the words that they have not circled.

Yes or No? Challenge students to change the true sentences to false sentences and vice versa.

Picture Match Ask students to make up their own sentences to describe the pictures.

What's the Question?
Challenge students to think of one or two new questions for each sentence.

Other Games and Conversation Exercises

The following games and exercises can add variety and energy to your classroom. They reinforce learning and capture students' attention through a lively, active medium. The games can be used with any of the chapters in *Let's Talk!* Feel free to invent your own variations and adapt them to your own classroom and students.

Friendly Feud

Make Hebrew word cards of the chapter's words. Divide the class into two teams, א and ב. One player from each team goes to the front of the room. Hold up a word card. The players raise their hands if they can use the word in a sentence. The student who raises a hand first gets a chance at answering. If the player says a correct sentence, that team gets two points. If the player is wrong, the other player gets to try; if correct, that team wins two points. If this second player also makes a mistake, all remaining students may raise their hands. In this follow-up round, the student who uses the word correctly wins one point for his or her team.

The team with the most points wins the game.

Around the World

Students sit on chairs in a circle. Student א is selected to be the first "world traveler" and stands behind a neighbor's chair (Student ב). Show a word card; if Student א reads it correctly first, that student moves one place around the circle. If Student ב reads it correctly first, Student ב switches places with Student א and attempts to be the one to go around the world — back to his or her original seat. Applaud the student who manages to go around the world, as well as a few more students who travel the furthest.

Hebrew Baseball

Using four chairs (one for each base), create a mock baseball diamond in your classroom. Divide the class into two teams and have them sit on opposite sides of the room. Choose a team to be at bat. That team will send one student at a time to home plate. That student will then choose the difficulty level of a question that he or she will answer: a single, double, triple, or home run. Prepare questions for each level in advance.

Sample questions include:

- For a single: What is the English translation of the word מָחָר? *(tomorrow)*
- For a double: In Hebrew, name three things you can wear. (*Answers may include:* בְּגָדִים, כּוֹבַע, כִּפָּה)
- For a triple: Answer the following question in Hebrew:

  מִי רוֹצָה לִקְנוֹת טַלִּית?

  (מַיָה רוֹצָה לִקְנוֹת טַלִּית.)
- For a home run: Say the Hebrew for "I like to play basketball with friends."

  (אֲנִי אוֹהֵב/אוֹהֶבֶת לְשַׂחֵק כַּדּוּרְסַל

  עִם חֲבֵרִים.)

If the student answers correctly, he or she advances the number of bases chosen (and anyone on base advances the same number of bases). If the student is incorrect, it's an out. Three outs, then the next team is at bat. Play as many innings as you'd like, but make sure the second team gets the final turn at bat.

Sentence Builders

Choose several simple sentences from a dialogue, making sure that a variety of pronouns and verb forms are represented. Write each word from these sentences on a separate index card. Give each student a card. Have students find other students with whom they can create a sentence. The first group that creates a grammatically correct sentence wins. Play several rounds with the same set of cards by simply shuffling and redistributing them.

Scrambled!

Give each student a blank sheet of paper and a pencil. Using a given set of words from a dialogue or activity, challenge students to create as many complete sentences as they can in five minutes.

After the time has expired, have each student read one sentence aloud. Determine whether the sentence is correct, based on gender and number. (אֲנִי לִשְׁתּוֹת and זֹאת כַּדּוּרְסַל, for example, are not, and therefore don't count.) Have all students with the same sentence cross theirs out.

Students receive points for unique sentences, based on the number of words in the sentence:

2 words. . . . . 1 point
3 words. . . . . 2 points
4 words. . . . . 3 points

The student with the most points at the end of the game is the winner.

Beat the Clock

Using a stopwatch or a watch with a second hand, time individual students as they read an assigned set of lines from a dialogue. Students should try to improve their own previous records. If a student makes a mistake, ask that student to read the word correctly before proceeding. Allow each student a maximum time of 60 seconds before proceeding to the next student. You may wish to challenge your students to reach a target time, perhaps 25 seconds.

Interview a Star

Invite several students to the front of the room. Assign each student the role of a character in the chapter's dialogue. Give each student a name tag or a prop to help classmates identify the character. Have the rest of the class interview the characters. You may wish to provide a few questions to begin the interview. For example, students may ask:

בֵּן, מָה אַתָּה אוֹהֵב לֶאֱכוֹל?

(Ben, what do you like to eat?)

The student who is role-playing Ben might answer:

אֲנִי אוֹהֵב לֶאֱכוֹל בּוּרִיטוֹ.

(I like to eat a burrito).

If possible, use a video camera to record the interviews. You may wish to have a "cast party" as you enjoy watching the video.

Stop!

Assign one or more students to read the dialog until they reach a specific word. For example, say: "Please read until you come to the Hebrew word for 'backpack'" or "Please read until you come to the Hebrew word for 'mountain.'" Ask the class to call out "Stop!" when the reader reaches the designated word. Then continue the game with other students.

Scope and Sequence Chart for *Let's Talk!*

Chapter	Dialogue	Page	Nouns	Verbs	Other
1	שָׁלוֹם	4			אֲנִי אַתְּ אַתָּה כֵּן לֹא מִי שָׁלוֹם
2	נוֹסְעִים לְיִשְׂרָאֵל	10	אַבָּא אִמָּא	נוֹסֵעַ/נוֹסַעַת נוֹסְעִים/נוֹסְעוֹת	אֲנַחְנוּ גַּם הִנֵּה וְ__, וַ__ לְ__ מִ__ שֶׁל שֶׁלִּי
3	מַה בַּתִּיק?	16	בְּגָדִים כּוֹבַע סַנְדָּלִים קִבּוּץ רֹאשׁ תּוֹדָה תִּיק		אֲבָל אֵין אֵין לִי בְּ__, בַּ__ גָּדוֹל, גְּדוֹלָה הַ__ יֵשׁ יֵשׁ לִי כִּי מַה עַכְשָׁו עַל

Chapter	Dialogue	Page	Nouns	Verbs	Other
4	מִי רוֹצֶה לֶאֱכוֹל?	22	חָלָב מַיִם מִיץ סוּכָּר עֲנָבִים פְּרִי, פֵּרוֹת קָפֶה תֵּה	לֶאֱכוֹל לִשְׁתּוֹת רוֹצֶה/רוֹצָה רוֹצִים/רוֹצוֹת	בְּבַקָּשָׁה עִם
5	לְהִתְרָאוֹת בְּתֵל-אָבִיב	28	אוֹטוֹבּוּס דוֹד/דוֹדָה יוֹם רְבִיעִי מוֹנִית מִשְׁפָּחָה, מִשְׁפָּחוֹת	לְהִתְרָאוֹת רוֹאֶה/רוֹאָה רוֹאִים/רוֹאוֹת	אֵיפֹה זֶה/זֹאת שֶׁלְּךָ/שֶׁלָּךְ
6	בַּקִּבּוּץ	34	בֵּית-כְּנֶסֶת בֵּית-סֵפֶר גַּן חָבֵר/חֲבֵרָה חֲבֵרִים/חֲבֵרוֹת חֲדַר-אֹכֶל	גָּר/גָּרָה גָּרִים/גָּרוֹת עוֹבֵד/עוֹבֶדֶת עוֹבְדִים/עוֹבְדוֹת	הַרְבֵּה כָּל קָטָן שֶׁלָּנוּ
7	בְּחֵיפָה	40	בַּיִת הַר חֶדֶר יֶלֶד/יַלְדָּה יְלָדִים כַּדּוּר כַּדּוּרֶגֶל כַּדּוּרְסַל	אוֹהֵב/אוֹהֶבֶת אוֹהֲבִים/אוֹהֲבוֹת לִרְאוֹת לְשַׂחֵק לָשִׂים	אַחֵר בְּסֵדֶר יָפֶה/יָפָה מַה שְׁלוֹמְךָ מַה שְׁלוֹמֵךְ טוֹב/טוֹבָה

Chapter	Dialogue	Page	Nouns	Verbs	Other
8	בִּירוּשָׁלַיִם	46	דֶּגֶל הַיּוֹם הַכֹּתֶל חֲנוּת טַלִּית כּוֹס קִדּוּשׁ כִּפָּה/כִּפּוֹת מָחָר צֶבַע תְּפִילָּה/תְּפִילּוֹת	לָלֶכֶת לִקְנוֹת צָרִיךְ/צְרִיכָה	כָּחוֹל כִּי לָבָן
9	בַּטֶּלֶפוֹן	52	בְּשָׁעָה מִסְפָּר שָׁעָה		אַחַת אֶפֶס אַרְבַּע חָמֵשׁ עַל-יַד עֶשֶׂר שֶׁבַע שָׁלֹשׁ שְׁמוֹנֶה שֵׁשׁ שְׁתַּיִם תֵּשַׁע
10	בְּתֵל-אָבִיב	58	אֹכֶל יוֹם חֲמִישִׁי מִסְעָדָה עוּגוֹת	אוֹכְלִים/אוֹכְלוֹת בָּא/בָּאָה בָּאִים/בָּאוֹת	אַתֶּם כְּמוֹ
11	בַּת-מִצְוָה בִּירוּשָׁלַיִם	64	בֶּן-דּוֹד בַּת-דּוֹדָה סַבָּא סַבְתָּא	לָשֶׁבֶת קוֹרֵא/קוֹרֵאת קוֹרְאִים/קוֹרְאוֹת שָׁר/שָׁרָה שָׁרִים/שָׁרוֹת	מַה שְׁלוֹמְכֶם מַזָּל טוֹב נָעִים מְאֹד

Chapter	Dialogue	Page	Nouns	Verbs	Other
12	בַּמִדְבָּר	70	בֶּגֶד-יָם גָמָל, גְמַלִים טִיוּל כֵּיף מִדְבָּר מָקוֹם	לִנְסוֹעַ	חַם מְאֹד
13	בְּאֵילַת	76	דָג, דָגִים יָם סִירָה		אָדוֹם אֶפְשָׁר יָפִים/יָפוֹת יָרוֹק צָהוֹב קַר
14	בְּיַם-הַמֶלַח	82	יוֹם שֵׁנִי יַם-הַמֶלַח מֶלַח מְצָדָה פֹּה עַתִּיקוֹת	לַעֲלוֹת לָשִׁיר	עוֹד עַתִּיק
15	לְהִתְרָאוֹת חֲבֵרִים!	88	אֲנָשִׁים מַתָּנָה, מַתָּנוֹת עִיר שׁוּק שִׁיר, שִׁירִים	קוֹנֶה/קוֹנָה קוֹנִים/קוֹנוֹת	יוֹפִי

Enrichment Ideas for Chapters

Chapter 1 • שָׁלוֹם

Welcome to *Let's Talk!*

Have students imagine that they are about to go on a trip to Israel. Ask which places they would like to visit and what things they would like to do while in Israel. List student responses on a large sheet of paper.

Explain to students that this year they will learn to speak Hebrew as they follow the journey of four young travelers to Israel. Give each student a copy of *Let's Talk!* Call on volunteers to describe in English the scenes depicted on the front and back covers. Read aloud the blurb on the back cover which describes the contents of the book. Have your class join you in reading the Hebrew phrase !נְסִיעָה טוֹבָה (Enjoy your journey!) Welcome them on their journey to Israel.

Tell your students that at the end of the year the class will compare the list of places they would like to visit to the places visited by the travelers in *Let's Talk!*

Introducing the Dialogue

Direct students to look at the illustrations on pages 4 and 5. Ask the following questions:

- Who is traveling? (דָּנִיאֵל, מַיָה, דִּינָה, בֵּן)
  Note: If students do not have labels for Dinah and Ben in the illustration on page 5, have them label the characters themselves.
- Where are they? *(in an airport)*
- Are they in Israel or the United States? *(United States)*
- How can you tell from the illustration? *(signs are only in English)*
- To which airline do the airplanes outside belong? *(El Al)*
  Explain to your class that while there are many airlines that fly to Israel, El Al was established in 1948 as the national airline of Israel.

Ask your students if they know how the travelers would say "hello" to each other in Hebrew. (שָׁלוֹם)

Welcome Board

Create a Welcome Board for your classroom. Write שָׁלוֹם כִּתָּה ו' (or whatever grade you teach) across the top of a large sheet of poster board. Ask each student to bring in a recent photo of him or herself. Give out pieces of construction paper and instruct students to mount the photo onto the construction paper. Then have students write a caption for their photo by completing the phrase

שָׁלוֹם. אֲנִי __________.

Encourage students to decorate the "frame" of their photographs. Have each student show his or her photo to the class and tell the class:

שָׁלוֹם. אֲנִי __________.

Mount all the framed photographs on the poster board. Display the Welcome Board in your classroom.

What's Your Name?

Have students sit in a circle. Using the name of one student, ask who that person is, for example, מִי טוֹבָה? That student (Tovah) responds by saying: אֲנִי טוֹבָה. Continue by having the first student (Tovah) ask about another student in the class. Continue until all students have had a turn asking מִי _______? and responding with אֲנִי _______. Applaud your students for speaking Hebrew.

Note: English names can be used instead of Hebrew.

Who Am I?

Place two chairs at the front of the classroom. Invite a student to sit on one of the chairs and blindfold him or her. Silently choose a second student and have that student sit on a chair next to the blindfolded student. The blindfolded student must guess who is sitting in the next chair. The "guesser" must ask: אַתָּה/אַתְּ _______? The second student responds with either כֵּן, אֲנִי _______ or לֹא, אֲנִי לֹא _______. Encourage students to use silly voices to disguise their identity. Allow the "guesser" three chances to correctly identify the other student. Invite two more students to the front of the room. If time allows, continue until all students have had a turn.

A World of Shalom

Explain to your students that the word שָׁלוֹם is from the root letters שׁלמ, meaning "completeness." Tell them that in the Bible, שָׁלוֹם has many meanings, for example:

completeness	safety	soundness
welfare	health	prosperity
peace	quiet	tranquility

Ask: What are the three meanings of שָׁלוֹם today? *(hello, good-bye, peace)*

Divide your class into groups of 4–6 students. Distribute siddurim to all students. Challenge them to find and list in five minutes as many songs and prayers — with their page numbers — containing the word שָׁלוֹם. *Answers may include:*

שָׁלוֹם עֲלֵיכֶם, שִׂים שָׁלוֹם, עוֹשֶׂה שָׁלוֹם, שָׁלוֹם רָב

Have one group read its list. Have all groups with the same song or prayer cross theirs out. Continue until all groups have read and compared their lists. The group with the most songs and prayers remaining on its list wins. If time permits, sing a few of these songs or invite the cantor to teach a song to your class.

Chapter 2 • נוֹסְעִים לְיִשְׂרָאֵל

Introducing the Dialogue

Tell students in Hebrew where you are from, saying: ____אֲנִי מִ. For example: אֲנִי מִנְיוּ גֶ'רְסִי (I am from New Jersey). Write ____מִ on the board. Continue by telling where a famous person comes from (for example: ג'וֹרְג' בּוּשׁ מִטֶקְסַס [George Bush is from Texas]). Ask: What do you think ____מִ means? *(from)* Call on each student to tell the class in Hebrew where he or she is from. After all students have spoken, explain that in this chapter Maya, her parents, and the other travelers will tell each other where they are from.

Using the Illustration

Before students hear the dialogue, direct them to look at the illustration on page 10. Ask:

- Who do you recognize in the illustration? *(Maya)*
- Who do you think is standing next to Maya? *(her parents)*
- Does anyone know how to say "father" in Hebrew? (אַבָּא)
- Does anyone know how to say "mother" in Hebrew? (אִמָא)
- Will Maya be traveling alone or with her parents? *(with her parents, you can see that her mother is also holding a ticket)*
- Who is walking onto the plane ahead of Maya? *(Ben, Daniel and Dinah)*
- How might Maya introduce herself in Hebrew to the woman taking tickets? (שָׁלוֹם, אֲנִי מַיָה)
- What characters may be in this dialogue? *(Maya, her parents, Ben, Daniel, and Dinah)*

Have students close their books and listen to you present the dialogue.

Thumbs Up or Thumbs Down

Using four index cards of the same color, make the following (verb) word cards:

נוֹסֵעַ נוֹסַעַת נוֹסְעִים נוֹסְעוֹת

Using index cards of another color, make the following (subject) word cards:

אֲנִי אַתָּה אַתְּ דָנִיאֵל דִינָה בֵּן מַיָה
אַבָּא אִמָא אֲנַחְנוּ בֵּן וְדָנִיאֵל
דִינָה וְדָנִיאֵל מַיָה וְדִינָה אַבָּא וְאִמָא

Place all the word cards face down. Ask one student to turn over one card of each color and to then read the cards aloud as a "sentence." The rest of the class should give a "thumbs up" if the words form a correct sentence (for example, אִמָא נוֹסַעַת) and a "thumbs down" if they do not form a correct sentence (for example, אֲנַחְנוּ נוֹסֵעַ). Continue until each student has had a turn to pick word cards and to read a new sentence.

Meeting at the Airport

Invite four students to the front of the room. Ask them to role play the following: They are four travelers meeting for the first time on their way to Israel and they are telling each other their names and where they are from. In a second scenario, invite another group of four students to the front. Assign each student one of the following parts: Ben, Maya, Maya's mother, and Maya's father. Ask these students to role-play Ben meeting Maya's family. You may wish to call up other groups of students and assign them the roles of different characters.

From Here to There

Write the following on the board:

____ (נוֹסֵעַ, נוֹסַעַת, נוֹסְעִים, נוֹסְעוֹת) מִ___ לְ___

Explain that you will say a starting word for this sentence and students will complete the sentence. For example, you might say: ______ שָׂרָה.

Completed sentences could include:

שָׂרָה נוֹסַעַת מִטוֹרוֹנְטוֹ לְלוֹס-אַנְגְ'לֶס.

שָׂרָה נוֹסַעַת מִקָנָדָה לְיִשְׂרָאֵל.

שָׂרָה נוֹסַעַת מִנְיוּ-יוֹרְק לְלוֹנְדוֹן.

Direct all students to stand. Say any pronoun that was taught in chapter 1 or 2, אַבָּא, אִמָּא, or a proper name, and ask a student to complete the sentence using that word. If the student says a correct sentence, he or she remains standing. If the student is unable to say a correct sentence, the student sits down. Continue going around the class, having students complete sentences. After all students have had a turn, those students who are standing are the winners.

Places of Origin

Give each student a 1" x 3" strip of white paper. Instruct students to write a sentence on the paper stating where they are from (for example, אֲנִי מִקְלִיבְלֶנְד). Mount these sentences below each student's photograph on the Welcome Board you created when studying chapter 1.

לֹא or כֵּן

Divide the class into two teams, א and ב. Read aloud a sentence from either chapter 1 or chapter 2. Call on a member of א to give an English translation of the sentence. The player may either give a correct translation or may bluff by giving an incorrect translation. Ask a player on team ב if the translation is correct. The player must respond כֵּן if the translation is correct or לֹא if the translation is incorrect. ב receives a point for accurately assessing if the translation was or was not correct. Continue the game by reading a Hebrew sentence to ב. Have a member of ב translate the sentence, ask א if the translation is correct, and have a member from א answer כֵּן or לֹא to assess the translation. Continue having teams take turns translating and saying if the translation is or is not accurate. The team with the most points is the winning team.

Variation: To earn an additional point, a team can give the accurate translation if the other team bluffed.

Using the Photographs

Call on a student to read the caption next to the photograph on page 11. Ask students to identify the airline. *(El Al)* Tell the class about Operation Solomon which took place in May 1991. Over a period of 36 hours, 14,324 Ethiopian Jews were rescued and resettled in Israel. Thirty-six El Al jumbo jets and transport planes had all their seats removed to allow for the greatest number of passengers to be brought to Israel. Over 1,000 Ethiopian Jews were airlifted on a single El Al Boeing 747!

Describe to your class — or have a student who has visited Israel do so — how all the passengers sing and clap when a plane lands in Israel.

Chapter 3 • מַה בַּתִּיק?

Introducing the Dialogue

Ask: If you were going to Israel what might you pack? *(Answers may include: hat, sunglasses, guide book, phone numbers of relatives or friends in Israel)* Explain that in this chapter we will listen in on a conversation that the travelers have about what they each packed in their backpacks.

Using the Illustration

Direct students to open to the illustration on page 16. Ask:

מִי נוֹסֵעַ לְיִשְׂרָאֵל?

Challenge your class to give at least ten answers.

Answers may include:

בֵּן נוֹסֵעַ לְיִשְׂרָאֵל.

מַיָה נוֹסַעַת לְיִשְׂרָאֵל.

מַיָה וְדִינָה נוֹסְעוֹת לְיִשְׂרָאֵל.

יֵשׁ לִי — אֵין לִי
I Have — I Don't Have

Ask students to stand in a circle. Hold a backpack and say יֵשׁ לִי תִּיק. Pass the backpack to the student next to you, say אֵין לִי תִּיק, and direct that student to say יֵשׁ לִי תִּיק. Continue having students pass the backpack around the circle until each student has had a turn. Hold a hat and say יֵשׁ לִי כּוֹבַע. Pass the hat to the next student, as you did the backpack, say אֵין לִי כּוֹבַע and have that student say: יֵשׁ לִי כּוֹבַע. Continue until all students have been given the hat.

Kibbutzim in Israel

Ask students to tell what they know about a kibbutz. List their responses on the board. You may also want to ask guiding questions such as: What is the difference between a kibbutz and a village? Where are kibbutzim located? Approximately how many kibbutzim are there? What are the main industries of kibbutzim? What jobs do people have on kibbutzim? Are kibbutzim today the same as they were thirty years ago?

For more information about kibbutzim, you can do research online, or you and the class can read and discuss the description of kibbutzim in *Welcome to Israel!* (Behrman House), pages 88-90. Ask students to write down at least one new thing they learned from the reading and to share it with their classmates.

Direct students to find pictures of kibbutzim — there are lots of great photos on the Internet — and to bring 2-3 pictures to your next class. Write the word קִבּוּץ in the center of a sheet of poster board. Have students mount their pictures on the poster board to create a collage about kibbutz life.

Being Contrary

Challenge students to disagree in Hebrew with each sentence that you say. Say a sentence from the dialogue and call on a student to say its opposite. Sample sentences and their opposites include:

- הַתִּיק שֶׁלִּי גָדוֹל. (הַתִּיק שֶׁלִּי לֹא גָדוֹל.)
- יֵשׁ בְּגָדִים. (אֵין בְּגָדִים.)
- אֵין לִי רֹאשׁ. (יֵשׁ לִי רֹאשׁ.)

Word Find

Distribute sheets of graph paper to students and ask them to create a Word Find which includes eight to ten of the new vocabulary words from chapter 3. Instruct students to list below the grid the English meaning of each of the Hebrew words in the Word Find. Have students switch with a partner and solve the partner's Word Find.

The Missing Word

Make word cards for the vocabulary of chapter 3. Have all students join you in reading the words aloud twice. Display 6–8 word cards. Divide the class into two teams, א and ב. Ask students to put their heads down on their desks and close their eyes while you remove one of the cards. Once the card is removed, tell students to look at the words on display. Call on a student from א to say which word is missing by completing the phrase ____ אֵין. The student must also give the English meaning of the missing word.

If the student answers correctly, א earns a point and the student is invited to add a new word card to the display. The student then removes another card while classmates have their eyes closed. If the student does not answer correctly, ב tries to identify and translate the word card. Continue by having teams take turns removing a card and guessing which card is missing. The team with the most points is the winning team.

What's in the Bag?

Direct students to look at the illustration on page 18. Ask: מַה בַּתִּיק? Have students respond in full Hebrew sentences.

מָצָאתִי! — I Found It!

Have students locate a word or phrase on page 16 or 17, based on clues that you provide.

Sample clues may include:

- Find the word for "backpack."
- Find the words that mean, "Now I have a hat."
- Find the place to which Dina is traveling.

Have students call מָצָאתִי! (I found it!) when they locate the word or phrase. The first student who calls מָצָאתִי! should read the word or phrase. If that student reads correctly, he or she receives a point. If that student does not, the other students have an opportunity to call מָצָאתִי! and read the word or phrase.

Using the Photograph

Have a student read the caption for the photograph on page 21. Ask:

- ► Do you think this store is in Israel or North America? *(Israel)*
- ► Why then is there a sign in English? *(There are many English speaking tourists in Israel who would not understand the sign in Hebrew.)*
- ► What do you think the weather is like where the store is located? *(Hot, the clothes look like summer clothing.)*

Going around the classroom, have each student give a יֵשׁ or אֵין sentence describing the photograph. *Sentences may include:*

יֵשׁ בְּגָדִים. • אֵין סַנְדָּלִים. • יֵשׁ תִּיק.

Introducing the Dialogue

Inform students that the flight from New York to Israel takes between ten and eleven hours. Ask: What are some things you would like to do on such a long flight? *(Answers may include: read, listen to music, watch a movie, eat, sleep)* Explain that in chapter 4 we will hear a conversation about what Maya, her parents, and her friends would like to eat and drink while on the airplane.

Using the Illustration

Ask students to look at the illustration on page 22 and to name in Hebrew the drinks the travelers will be offered on their flight.

(מַיִם, קוֹלָה, תֵּה, קָפֶה, מִיץ)

Sentence Whip

Begin by saying: .אֲנִי רוֹצָה לֶאֱכוֹל בַּנָּנָה

Pause, and then say: רוֹצֶה.

Call on a student to create a new sentence by replacing a word in the sentence with רוֹצֶה.

The student should say: .אֲנִי רוֹצֶה לֶאֱכוֹל בַּנָּנָה

Repeat the student's sentence and say a new replacement word or phrase, such as לִשְׁתּוֹת חָלָב.

Again, call on a student to create a new sentence with the phrase לִשְׁתּוֹת חָלָב.

Continue the whip until all students have had a turn.

Blessing Posters

Create a poster for blessings recited over different foods and drinks. Include all the foods and drinks mentioned in the chapter. Write or mount the ending words for each of the following blessings on poster board.

הַמּוֹצִיא לֶחֶם מִן הָאָרֶץ
bread

שֶׁהַכֹּל נִהְיֶה בִּדְבָרוֹ
candy, soup, meat, chicken, fish, eggs, most drinks

בּוֹרֵא מִינֵי מְזוֹנוֹת
foods made from grain that are not breads

בּוֹרֵא פְּרִי הַגָּפֶן
wine or grape juice

בּוֹרֵא פְּרִי הָעֵץ
most fruits

בּוֹרֵא פְּרִי הָאֲדָמָה
vegetables, legumes, and certain fruits
(bananas, melons, pineapple, some berries)

Have students cut out pictures of various foods from magazines. Mount the pictures on the poster board next to their blessing endings.

Commercial Time

Divide the class into groups of 3–4 students. Assign each group a food or drink, such as פֵּרוֹת or חָלָב. Direct the groups to compose a song advertising their food. The song can be a mixture of Hebrew and English words. Encourage students to use as many Hebrew words as possible. Have each group present its ad to the class. Students may also want to draw illustrations or make props related to their advertisement.

Using the Photograph

Ask students to look at the photograph on page 24 and to read the caption aloud. Ask if the foods mentioned in chapter 4 are found on the tray in the photograph. For example:

יֵשׁ פֵּרוֹת לֶאֱכֹל? (כֵּן, יֵשׁ פֵּרוֹת לֶאֱכֹל.)

יֵשׁ חָלָב לִשְׁתּוֹת? (לֹא, אֵין חָלָב לִשְׁתּוֹת.)

Eat and Drink

Have students sit in a circle. Explain that each student will be asked either:

מַה אַתָּה/אַתְּ רוֹצֶה/רוֹצָה לֶאֱכוֹל?

מַה אַתָּה/אַתְּ רוֹצֶה/רוֹצָה לִשְׁתּוֹת? or

The first student answers, for example,

אֲנִי רוֹצֶה לֶאֱכוֹל עֲנָבִים.

then asks the next student what he or she would like to eat or drink. That student needs to say what the first student wants and then what he or she wants, for example:

דָנִי רוֹצֶה לֶאֱכוֹל עֲנָבִים. אֲנִי רוֹצָה לִשְׁתּוֹת קוֹלָה.

Continue going around the circle, having a student say what each of the other students wants, and then answering for him or herself. If a student fails to repeat what others have said, that student moves slightly back from the circle. The students remaining in the circle after everyone has had a turn are the winners.

Tic-Tac-Toe on the Go

Arrange nine chairs in three rows of three chairs each. Prepare ten strips of paper — five white and five blue — to use as "markers" for each tic-tac-toe spot. Divide the class into two teams — לָבָן (white) and כָּחוֹל (blue). Give the strips of paper to the students.

Say any Hebrew vocabulary word from chapters 1–4. Ask a student from the לָבָן team to say the English meaning of the word. If the student gives a correct translation, he or she may choose to sit — with the team's "marker" — in any of the nine chairs. Then ask a student from the כָּחוֹל team the meaning of another Hebrew word. If that student answers correctly, he or she may choose to sit in any of the other chairs. The team that gets three in a row, in any direction, wins.

To make this even more challenging, say a phrase or sentence in Hebrew and ask students to translate it.

Connecting Words

Write the following on the board:

בְּ___ אֲבָל הַ___ מִ___ וְ___ לְ___ עִם גַּם

Have students work with a partner. Challenge the pairs to write eight sentences. Each sentence should contain one of the words or prefixes listed on the board.

Call on students to read their sentences aloud. Students receive a point for each correct sentence. The pair with the most points wins.

Extra challenge: For additional points, have students write compound sentences using more than one word or prefix.

Chapter 5 • לְהִתְרָאוֹת בְּתֵל-אָבִיב

Introducing the Dialogue

Write the names of the following cities on the board:

יְרוּשָׁלַיִם, חֵיפָה, תֵּל-אָבִיב

Ask:

- What are the English names for each of these cities. *(Jerusalem, Haifa and Tel Aviv)*
- What do you know about Tel Aviv? *(Answers may include: it is modern, it has lots of shopping and entertainment, it is on the Mediterranean Sea)*
- What do you know about Haifa? *(Answers may include: it is a beautiful city set up high on a mountain, there are both a cable car and a train [subway] that take you up and down the mountain, it is on the Mediterranean Sea)*
- What do you know about Jerusalem? *(Answers may include: it is the Holy City for Jews, Christians, and Muslims, it is the capital of Israel, in Jerusalem you can visit the Western Wall, it is the home of Hebrew University, it has an old and a new city)*

Explain that in this chapter the travelers tell each other which of these cities they will be visiting.

Using the Illustration

After students are familiar with the dialogue and the new vocabulary, ask them to look at the illustration on page 28. Ask questions based on the dialogue and the illustration such as:

- אֵיפֹה מַיָה? (מַיָה בַּמוֹנִית.)
- מִי לֹא בָּאוֹטוֹבּוּס וְגַם לֹא בַּמוֹנִית?
(דָנִיאֵל לֹא בָּאוֹטוֹבּוּס וְגַם לֹא בַּמוֹנִית.)
- מִי נוֹסֵעַ לַקִבּוּץ? (בֵּן וְדִינָה נוֹסְעִים לַקִבּוּץ.)

זֶה or זֹאת?

Tell students that nouns and adjectives in Hebrew are either masculine or feminine. Most nouns ending in הָ or ת are feminine. For feminine nouns, we use זֹאת (this is). For masculine nouns, we use זֶה.

Divide the class into four groups. Challenge groups to write as many correct זֶה or זֹאת sentences as they can in the next three minutes. When time is up, have each group read its list aloud. Ask others to raise their hands if they hear an incorrect sentence. If a sentence is incorrect, direct the group to correct the sentence. Have all groups join you in applauding others after they read their list of correct sentences.

Travel Posters

Divide the class into three groups. Have each group create a travel poster about Jerusalem, Haifa, or Tel Aviv. Travel brochures, magazines, newspapers, and the Internet are good sources for photographs of and information about sites in these cities.

Israel Geography

Display a map of Israel. Ask students to locate the places in Israel that they have read about in *Let's Talk!* You may need to help the students locate the following places:

Ben-Gurion International Airport	Haifa חֵיפָה
Tel-Aviv תֵּל-אָבִיב	Jerusalem יְרוּשָׁלַיִם

Have students place a Post-it® with the name of each place at its proper location. Explain that we do not know the location of the kibbutz mentioned in the dialogue.

מִי? מַה? אֵיפֹה?

Divide class into two teams, א and ב. Say a sentence that includes new vocabulary words, such as דָּנִיאֵל בַּמּוֹנִית. The א team must ask a question that the sentence answers (for example, מִי בַּמּוֹנִית? or אֵיפֹה דָּנִיאֵל?). א receives a point for asking a correct question. Continue having teams take turns asking questions. The team with the most points wins.

Where Is Your Family?

Tell students where your family is, saying:

הַמִּשְׁפָּחָה שֶׁלִּי בְּ____.

Turn to a student and ask:

אֵיפֹה הַמִּשְׁפָּחָה שֶׁלְּךָ/שֶׁלָּךְ?

After the student responds

הַמִּשְׁפָּחָה שֶׁלִּי בְּ____.

prompt that student to ask another student where his or her family is. Continue until all students have had a turn to both answer and ask this question.

Vary this activity by asking about an aunt or uncle:

אֵיפֹה הַדּוֹד שֶׁלְּךָ/שֶׁלָּךְ?

or אֵיפֹה הַדּוֹדָה שֶׁלְּךָ/שֶׁלָּךְ?

What Do You See?

Ask students if they see different things or people in the classroom. Questions may include:

- אַתָּה/אַתְּ רוֹאֶה/רוֹאָה מוֹנִית?
- אַתָּה/אַתְּ רוֹאֶה/רוֹאָה תִּיק?
- אַתָּה/אַתְּ רוֹאֶה/רוֹאָה אוֹטוֹבּוּס?
- אַתָּה/אַתְּ רוֹאֶה/רוֹאָה אֶת שָׂרָה?

Students should answer in full sentences.

אֶת or no אֶת?

Write the following on the board:

אֲנִי רוֹאֶה כּוֹבַע.

אֲנִי רוֹאֶה אֶת הַכּוֹבַע.

אֲנִי רוֹאֶה אֶת מַיָה.

Have the class read all three sentences in unison. Explain when a sentence does or does not need אֶת. (אֶת comes before a proper noun or a noun with the prefix הַ.) Do a sentence whip around the room replacing the ending noun. Each student will say a sentence using a noun that may or may not be preceded by אֶת.

Ask all students to stand at their seats. Say:

אֲנִי רוֹאֶה/רוֹאָה כּוֹבַע. קִבּוּץ.

The first student should now say:

אֲנִי רוֹאֶה/רוֹאָה קִבּוּץ.

The student remains standing if he or she has said the sentence correctly but sits if the sentence was not correct. The last student to remain standing is the winner. Replacement nouns include:

מַיָה, בֵּן, דָּנִיאֵל, דִּינָה, אַבָּא, נְיוּ-יוֹרְק, טוֹרוֹנְטוֹ,
(הַ)תִּיק, (הַ)קִּבּוּץ, (הַ)סַנְדָּלִים, (הַ)כּוֹבַע,
(הַ)בְּגָדִים, (הָ)רֹאשׁ, (הַ)פֵּרוֹת, (הָ)עֲנָבִים

Using the Photograph

Ask students to turn to the photo on page 30 (page is unmarked) and to read the caption in unison. Ask if they can guess what building they are looking at *(the main building at Ben Gurion International Airport)*. Have students join you in reading the English and Hebrew words that are on the building. Teach them that we welcome people by saying בְּרוּכִים הַבָּאִים (plural). Ask three students to go out of the classroom and to immediately reenter. When they return, have their classmates welcome them with a rousing בְּרוּכִים הַבָּאִים.

Chapter 6 • בַּקִּבּוּץ

Introducing the Dialogue

Ask your students: If you were going to a kibbutz, what are some things you would want to know in advance? List students' responses on the board. Inform students that in this chapter we will listen in as Dinah and Ben ask questions about the kibbutz they are visiting. We'll see if Dinah and Ben want to know any of the things that we listed on the board.

Using the Illustration

After students are familiar with the dialogue and the new vocabulary, have them look at the illustration on pages 34–35. Invite a student to the front of the room to ask classmates questions about the illustration. Questions and answers may include:

- מִי אַתָּה/אַתְּ רוֹאֶה/רוֹאָה? (גִּלְעָד, דִּינָה, בֵּן)
- מַה אַתָּה/אַתְּ רוֹאֶה/רוֹאָה? (תִּיק, קִבּוּץ, בֵּית-כְּנֶסֶת)
- יֵשׁ בֵּית-כְּנֶסֶת? (כֵּן, יֵשׁ בֵּית-כְּנֶסֶת.)

Concentration

Create one set of 5" x 7" index cards with the new Hebrew words from chapter 6, and one set of cards with their English translations. All cards should be blank on one side. Combine both sets and shuffle together. Place all cards, word-side up, on the floor or a large table. Then turn the cards over so that the blank side faces up. Ask students individually (or in teams) to try to match the Hebrew and English word pairs by turning any two cards over.

If the cards match, award the player or team a point and remove the matched pair of cards. If they do not match, place the cards back in their original position and ask another student (or the other team) to go. Continue the game until all cards have been removed. The player or team with the most points wins.

Mime the Line

Ask a student to come to the front of the room and show him or her a line from the dialogue. Direct the student to mime the line. The rest of the class should guess which line that student is acting out. The student who guesses the correct line and reads it accurately comes to the front of the room and acts out a different line that you identify.

Visiting a Kibbutz

Invite three students to the front of the room. Assign one student the role of a person who lives on a kibbutz and assign the other two the roles of visitors to the kibbutz. Have them role-play their first meeting at the kibbutz.

שָׁלוֹם חֲבֵרִים

Ask the class if they know the song שָׁלוֹם חֲבֵרִים.

שָׁלוֹם חֲבֵרִים, שָׁלוֹם חֲבֵרִים, שָׁלוֹם, שָׁלוֹם,
לְהִתְרָאוֹת, לְהִתְרָאוֹת, שָׁלוֹם, שָׁלוֹם.

If they already know the song, call on a student to lead the class. If not, invite your music teacher or cantor to teach the song. Challenge your students to translate the song into English.

Where We Live and Where We Work

Tell your students the cities or towns in which you live and work. Say:

אֲנִי גָר/גָרָה בְּ____ וַאֲנִי עוֹבֵד/עוֹבֶדֶת בְּ____.

אֵיפֹה חָבֵר/חֲבֵרָה שֶׁלְךָ/שֶׁלָךְ עוֹבֵד/עוֹבֶדֶת?
(חָבֵר/חֲבֵרָה שֶׁלִי עוֹבֵד/עוֹבֶדֶת בְּ____.)

אֵיפֹה הַמִשְׁפָּחָה שֶׁלְךָ/שֶׁלָךְ גָרָה?
(הַמִשְׁפָּחָה שֶׁלִי גָרָה בְּ____.)

Students can answer about an imaginary חָבֵר or חֲבֵרָה, and the response may be humorous. Have each student turn to a partner and ask the above questions. Remind the class that we use a feminine singular, not a plural, verb with מִשְׁפָּחָה. Call on students to tell the class where their partner's friend works and where the family lives.

Being Contrary

Challenge students to disagree in Hebrew with each sentence that you say. Say sentences that include new vocabulary words as well as words from previous chapters. *Sample sentences and their opposites may include:*

- זֶה בֵּית-סֵפֶר גָדוֹל. (לֹא, זֶה בֵּית-סֵפֶר קָטָן.)
- הַבְּגָדִים שֶׁלִי. (לֹא, הַבְּגָדִים שֶׁלָנוּ.)
- הַחֲבֵרִים גָרִים בַּקִבּוּץ.
  (לֹא, הַחֲבֵרִים גָרִים בִּירוּשָׁלַיִם.)

Fruits from Israel

Ask students if they have ever been to a fruit orchard. What type of fruit was grown? Explain that many kibbutzim have fruit orchards. Plan a גַן-פֵּרוֹת party during which you will serve fruits that grow in Israel. If possible, purchase Israeli products. Choose from the following list:

fig תְּאֵנָה — almond שָׁקֵד — pomegranate רִמוֹן
pear אַגָס — orange תַּפּוּז — peach אֲפַרְסֵק
olive זַיִת — carob חָרוּב — grapefruit אֶשְׁכּוֹלִית
date תָּמָר — banana בַּנָנָה — apple תַּפּוּחַ

Place each food in a dish with its Hebrew name on display.

Ask students, for example:

מִי רוֹצֶה/רוֹצָה לֶאֱכוֹל זַיִת?

Have students answer in Hebrew:

אֲנִי רוֹצֶה/רוֹצָה לֶאֱכוֹל זַיִת.

You may also want to serve apple juice (מִיץ תַּפּוּחִים) and orange juice (מִיץ תַּפּוּזִים).

Ask students:

מַה אַתָּה/אַתְּ רוֹצֶה/רוֹצָה לִשְׁתּוֹת?
(אֲנִי רוֹצֶה/רוֹצָה לִשְׁתּוֹת מִיץ תַּפּוּזִים.)

Using the Photograph

Have the class chorally read the caption next to the photograph on page 37.

Ask:

- What are some things you know about the kibbutz by looking at this picture? *(Answers may include: It is hot [the boy is wearing summer clothing], there are probably animals [the boy is wheeling a cart full of hay], children help out with chores)*
- Would you like to do this kind of work? Why or why not?
- What are some questions you would like to ask the boy about life on a kibbutz?

Chapter 7 • בְּחֵיפָה

Introducing the Dialogue

Ask students which sports they like to play. Then tell them that in this dialogue we will see how sports help to establish a connection between Daniel and his Israeli cousin, Gil.

Using the Illustration

Direct students to look at the illustration on page 40. Ask:

• מָה אַתָּה/אַתְּ רוֹאֶה/רוֹאָה?

Answers may include:

בַּיִת, כַּדּוּרֶגֶל, כּוֹבַע, הַר

• מִי אַתָּה/אַתְּ רוֹאֶה/רוֹאָה?

Answers may include:

דּוֹד, דּוֹדָה, גִּיל, דָּנִיאֵל

- What do you think Daniel might be saying in Hebrew?
- What do you think Gil might be saying in Hebrew?

Answers may include:

אַתָּה רוֹצֶה לְשַׂחֵק כַּדּוּרֶגֶל?
זֶה הַכַּדּוּר שֶׁלִּי.
אֲנִי רוֹצֶה כַּדּוּר.

The Missing Word

Make word cards for the vocabulary from chapter 7. Divide the class into two teams, א and ב. Place eight cards on the ledge of the board. Allow the class 15 seconds to look at the words. Ask students to put their heads down on their desks and close their eyes while you remove one of the cards. Call on a student from א to guess which word was removed, to say its meaning, and to use the word in a sentence. א earns one point for guessing the missing word, one more point for saying the correct meaning, and a third point for using the word correctly in a sentence. If א does not earn the full three points, ב gets to try to earn these points.

Show the class a new word card and place it on the ledge with the remaining seven cards. Again, remove a card while students are not looking. ב takes a turn and tries to earn three points. Continue having the teams take turns. The team with the most points wins. To make this game more challenging, change the order of the remaining cards or increase the number of cards on the ledge.

Picture This

Invite a student to the board. Point to one of the new vocabulary words on page 41 and direct the student to illustrate the word. Have the class guess the word. The first student who guesses correctly is then invited to the board, shown a new word, and asked to illustrate the word for others to guess.

Peace through Sports

Tell the class that both basketball and soccer are played in Israel to promote peace between Israelis and Palestinians. The Peres Center for Peace has twinned Israeli and Palestinian schools so that school children play basketball and soccer on mixed Palestinian-Israeli teams. In this project the students receive "Education for Values of Peace." A second organization, "Playing for Peace," has teamed up with the Peres Center to establish a year-round basketball program in Israel and the West Bank to improve relationships between Israeli and Palestinian youth.

Ask:

- Why do you think these organizations have chosen basketball and soccer as tools to help promote peace?
- What other types of activities or programs might be used to promote peace in Israel?

How Are You?

Turn to a male student and ask: מַה שְׁלוֹמְךָ? Prompt the student to respond: טוֹב, תּוֹדָה. Have students take turns asking the person next to them: מַה שְׁלוֹמְךָ? מַה שְׁלוֹמֵךְ? and then having that student respond with טוֹב, תּוֹדָה. Continue around the room until all students have had a turn.

Soccer or Basketball?

Invite two students to the front of the room. Give one a soccer ball and the other a basketball. Direct them to role-play a scene about deciding to play either soccer or basketball.

Sports Survey

Write on the board:

כַּדוּרֶגֶל וְגַם כַּדוּרְסַל?
לֹא כַּדוּרֶגֶל וְלֹא כַּדוּרְסַל?
כַּדוּרֶגֶל?
כַּדוּרְסַל?

Ask: • מִי אוֹהֵב לְשַׂחֵק כַּדוּרֶגֶל?

Call on each student whose hand is raised to respond:

(גַּם) אֲנִי אוֹהֵב/אוֹהֶבֶת לְשַׂחֵק כַּדוּרֶגֶל.

and ask those students to walk to one corner of the room.

Ask: • מִי אוֹהֵב לְשַׂחֵק כַּדוּרְסַל?

(גַּם) אֲנִי אוֹהֵב/אוֹהֶבֶת לְשַׂחֵק כַּדוּרְסַל.

Direct these students to a second corner of the room.

Ask:

• מִי אוֹהֵב לְשַׂחֵק כַּדוּרְסַל וְגַם אוֹהֵב לְשַׂחֵק כַּדוּרֶגֶל?

אֲנִי אוֹהֵב/אוֹהֶבֶת לְשַׂחֵק כַּדוּרֶגֶל וְגַם אוֹהֵב/אוֹהֶבֶת לְשַׂחֵק כַּדוּרְסַל.

Have these students go to another corner of the room.

Ask:

• מִי לֹא אוֹהֵב לְשַׂחֵק כַּדוּרְסַל וְגַם לֹא אוֹהֵב לְשַׂחֵק כַּדוּרֶגֶל?

אֲנִי לֹא אוֹהֵב/אוֹהֶבֶת לְשַׂחֵק כַּדוּרֶגֶל וַאֲנִי לֹא אוֹהֵב/אוֹהֶבֶת לְשַׂחֵק כַּדוּרְסַל.

Send these students to the last corner of the room.

Challenge each group to say five sentences based on the survey. *Sentences may include:*

הַרְבֵּה יְלָדִים אוֹהֲבִים לְשַׂחֵק כַּדוּרְסַל.
שָׂרָה וְדָנָה אוֹהֲבוֹת לְשַׂחֵק כַּדוּרֶגֶל.
אָבִי אוֹהֵב לְשַׂחֵק כַּדוּרֶגֶל.

Using the Photograph

Call on a student to read the caption below the photograph on page 43. Ask:

• מַה עַל הַר הַכַּרְמֶל? (הַבַּיִת)
• אֵיפֹה הַר הַכַּרְמֶל? (בְּחֵיפָה)

Ask students to imagine that they are one of the people in the photo looking out onto the city. Ask for volunteers to describe what they see and how they feel as they are looking at the view.

Introducing the Dialogue

Ask:

- Will any of you receive a special tallit or kippah for your bar or bat mitzvah ceremony? What makes it special? *(Answers may include: it was given to me by my aunt and uncle, it comes from Israel, my grandmother made it for me)*
- Will you be buying or receiving items from Israel for your bar or bat mitzvah?
- What other special things might you get for your bar or bat mitzvah ceremony? *(Answers may include: candlesticks, yad [pointer for the Torah], kiddush cup)*

Tell your students that in this chapter we will join Maya and her parents as they make a purchase in Jerusalem for Maya's bat mitzvah ceremony.

Using the Illustration

Direct students to look at the illustration on page 46. Ask questions, such as the following, based on the illustrations:

- מַה בַּחֲנוּת? (בַּחֲנוּת יֵשׁ טַלִּית, חֲנוּכִּיָּה, כִּפּוֹת, מְזוּזָה, כּוֹס קִדּוּשׁ, וְדֶגֶל יִשְׂרָאֵל.)
- מַה מַיָה רוֹצָה לִקְנוֹת? (מַיָה רוֹצָה לִקְנוֹת טַלִּית.)
- מִי בַּחֲנוּת? (מַיָה, אַבָּא, וְאִמָּא בַּחֲנוּת.)
- הַחֲנוּת יָפָה? (כֵּן, הַחֲנוּת יָפָה.)

A Frequent Request

Challenge students to say in Hebrew: Please put a kippah on (your) head.

(בְּבַקָּשָׁה לָשִׂים כִּפָּה עַל הָרֹאשׁ.)

Make a Mizraḥ

Show your students photographs of the *Kotel*, the Western Wall. Explain that the *Kotel* (short for *Kotel Ha'ma'aravi*, the Western Wall) is part of the retaining wall of the Second Temple, which was destroyed by the Romans in 70 C.E. Ask: Which direction is the *Kotel* from here? *(east)* Write the word מִזְרָח on the board and explain that it means "east." Explain that a מִזְרָח is a decoration hung on an eastern wall and that it reminds us to face east, toward the *Kotel*, while praying.

Have your class create one large מִזְרָח for your classroom. Print מִזְרָח in the center of a sheet of poster board. Ask students to draw pictures that remind them of Jerusalem. They can also cut out illustrations or photos from magazines, newspapers, and travel catalogs. Have students mount the illustrations or photos onto poster board to create a collage מִזְרָח. Display the מִזְרָח on the eastern wall of your classroom.

Time to Shop

Divide the class into three groups. Assign each group a different type of store: a Judaica shop, a department store, or a snack bar. Designate one person in each group to be the storekeeper and the others to be the customers. Explain that each group will role-play a scene that could take place in the assigned store. Allow groups five minutes to prepare a skit. Have props available to make the skits fun and lively. Call each group to the front of the room to present its skit.

Scrambled!

Give each student a blank sheet of paper and a pencil. Challenge the students to create as many complete sentences as they can in five minutes, using at least two new vocabulary words from chapter 8 in each sentence along with words from previous chapters.

After the time has expired, have each student read one sentence aloud. Together, determine whether the sentence is correct, based on gender and number. (אֲנִי לִקְנוֹת and לָלֶכֶת הַכֹּתֶל, for example, are not correct, and therefore don't count.) Have all students with the same sentence cross theirs out.

Students receive points for unique correct sentences, based on the number of words in the sentence:

2 words . . . . 1 point
3 words . . . . 2 points
4 words . . . . 3 points

The student with the most points at the end of the game is the winner.

Blue and White

Invite the music teacher or the cantor to teach your class כָּחוֹל וְלָבָן by Israel Reshel.

כָּחוֹל וְלָבָן, זֶה הַצֶּבַע שֶׁלִּי;
כָּחוֹל וְלָבָן, צִבְעֵי אַדְמָתִי.
כָּחוֹל וְלָבָן, כָּחוֹל וְלָבָן, זֶה הַצֶּבַע שֶׁלִּי,
כָּל יָמַי, לְעוֹלָם.

Blue and white, that's my color;
blue and white, the colors of my land.
Blue and white, blue and white, that's my color,
all my days, forever.

What Do You Need to Buy?

Create word cards for the nouns from chapter 8 as well as for nouns from previous chapters.

Give each student a word card. Begin by holding up the word card for דֶּגֶל and saying:

אֲנִי צָרִיךְ/צְרִיכָה לָלֶכֶת לִקְנוֹת דֶּגֶל.

As you say דֶּגֶל act out a motion, such as waving a flag, that reflects the meaning of your word.

Call on a student and ask:

מַה אֲנִי צָרִיךְ/צְרִיכָה לָלֶכֶת לִקְנוֹת?
(אַתָּה/אַתְּ צָרִיךְ/צְרִיכָה לָלֶכֶת לִקְנוֹת דֶּגֶל.)

Be sure the student repeats your motions when saying דֶּגֶל. Then ask the student:

מַה אַתָּה/אַתְּ צָרִיךְ/צְרִיכָה לָלֶכֶת לִקְנוֹת?

The student answers by using his or her word in a sentence and acting out the word.

Prompt that student to then ask another student:

מַה אֲנִי צָרִיךְ/צְרִיכָה לָלֶכֶת לִקְנוֹת?
מַה אַתָּה/אַתְּ צָרִיךְ/צְרִיכָה לָלֶכֶת לִקְנוֹת?

Continue until all students have said what they as well as a fellow student need to go buy.

Using the Photograph

Have a student read the caption next to the photo on page 51. Ask students to answer the questions from the caption. Have them describe the photograph in Hebrew. *(Answers may include:*
הַחֲנוּת לֹא גְּדוֹלָה, חֲנוּכִּיָּה בַּחֲנוּת, הַחֲנוּת יָפָה)

Have a student read the "Big Discount" sign. Ask: Why would a store owner hang a sign like this? What can we do to help store owners in Israel? Explain that tourism is an important part of Israel's economy. Even when we are not in Israel we can support its economy by buying products made in Israel in our own stores as well as on the Internet.

Chapter 9 • בְּטֶלֶפוֹן

Introducing the Dialogue

Ask:

אֵיפֹה מַיָה? (בִּירוּשָׁלַיִם)
אֵיפֹה בֵּן וְדִינָה? (בַּקִּבּוּץ)
אֵיפֹה דָנִיאֵל? (בְּחֵיפָה)

Where did the friends plan to meet one another? *(Tel Aviv)*

Tell students that in this dialogue we will overhear a phone conversation during which the travelers finalize their plans to meet in Tel Aviv.

Using the Illustration

Invite students to look at the illustrations on pages 52 and 53. Point to the illustration of Ben, and ask:

מַה רוֹצֶה בֵּן?

Answers may include:

בֵּן רוֹצֶה אֶת מִסְפַּר הַטֶלֶפוֹן שֶׁל מַיָה.
בֵּן רוֹצֶה לִרְאוֹת אֶת מַיָה.
בֵּן רוֹצֶה לֶאֱכוֹל פִּיצָה.

Continue by pointing to the illustrations of the other characters and asking:

מַה רוֹצֶה דָנִיאֵל? מַה רוֹצָה מַיָה?

Bounce and Count

Challenge students to bounce a ball ten times and to count the number of bounces from אַחַת to עֶשֶׂר. For an extra challenge, ask students to count backwards (from עֶשֶׂר to אַחַת), saying the next number with each bounce of the ball.

What's Your Phone Number?

Give each student a piece of paper. Call on one student and ask:

מַה מִסְפַּר הַטֶלֶפוֹן שֶׁלְךָ/שֶׁלָךְ?

As the student responds, for example,

מִסְפַּר הַטֶלֶפוֹן שֶׁלִי
חָמֵשׁ, חָמֵשׁ, אֶפֶס, שֵׁשׁ, אַחַת, שָׁלֹשׁ, שֵׁשׁ

the classmates write those numerals on their papers. The student then writes his or her phone number on the board. Each student who has correctly written the phone number receives a point.

Continue going around room, asking each student to say his or her phone number aloud in Hebrew while others write the number on their own paper. Continue until everyone has had a turn.

The students with the most points are the winners.

My Favorite Time

Create a "בְּשָׁעָה ___ אֲנִי אוֹהֵב/אוֹהֶבֶת לְ___" bulletin board. Invite students to complete the sentence out loud telling the class about something they like to do at a certain time. Write the sentences on the board. *Sentences may include:*

בְּשָׁעָה שָׁלֹשׁ אֲנִי אוֹהֵב לְשַׂחֵק כַּדּוּרֶגֶל.
בְּשָׁעָה אַחַת אֲנִי אוֹהֶבֶת לֶאֱכוֹל פִּיצָה.

Give students each a sheet of construction paper and instruct them to write a sentence telling about something they like to do at a certain time and to illustrate the activity. If students are not able to fully describe the activity in Hebrew, they can write a part in Hebrew and then illustrate the activity. Encourage students to use infinitives they learned in previous chapters.

Sudoku

Have students work with a partner. Make copies of an easy-level Sudoku number placement puzzle using the numbers one to nine, and give a copy to each pair of students. Challenge students to complete the puzzle, speaking רַק עִבְרִית! The first pair to complete the puzzle is the winner.

Go Fish

Divide the class into groups of three to six students. Prepare a set of cards for each group by taking a standard 52-card deck and removing all the Jacks, Queens and Kings. Give each group a deck of forty cards.

To Play: Deal five cards to each player and place the remaining cards face down in a draw pile. The first player asks another player in Hebrew if he or she has a specific number card. For example:

יוֹנָה, יֵשׁ לְךָ עֶשֶׂר?

The asker must already hold a card with this number.

If the player asked has any cards of the requested number, that player must say כֵּן and give all of those cards to the asker. (יוֹנָה would have to give the first player all of his tens.) The asker then goes again.

If the person asked has no cards for the number requested, that person says לֹא and the asker draws the top card from the draw pile.

If the player happens to draw a card of the number asked for, the asker keeps the card and asks again. If the card that is drawn is not a card of the number asked for, the asker keeps the card but it becomes the next player's turn. The next player is the one who said לֹא.

When a player collects a set of four cards of the same number, that player must immediately show the set to the other players, say which set has been collected (יֵשׁ לִי עֶשֶׂר), and place the four cards face down in front of him or herself.

The game continues until either someone has no cards left or the draw pile runs out. The winner is the player who then has the most sets of four.

Beat the Clock

Have your class work together to beat a target time. Announce to the class that you are challenging them to read the dialogue for chapter 9 correctly in under three minutes. Ask each student to read one line in turn. If the class beats the target time, have the students repeat the lines, and try to beat a new target time.

Note: Allow students to opt out if they do not want to participate in this timed exercise.

Telling Time

Bring a clock to class. Set the time to one o'clock and say הַשָּׁעָה אַחַת. Have students repeat the time. Change the time to two o'clock, say הַשָּׁעָה שְׁתַּיִם, and have students repeat. Change the time to three o'clock and ask: מַה הַשָּׁעָה? (הַשָּׁעָה שָׁלֹשׁ) Invite two students to the front of the room. Direct one student to change the clock to any hour from one o'clock to ten o'clock. Have the second student ask מַה הַשָּׁעָה? and call on classmates to respond.

Enrichment: Teach the class the numbers eleven (אַחַת-עֶשְׂרֵה) and twelve (שְׁתֵּים-עֶשְׂרֵה).

Extra enrichment: Talk about time differences between your city and Israel. *For example:*

הַשָּׁעָה בְּנְיוּ-יוֹרְק שָׁלֹשׁ. מַה הַשָּׁעָה בְּיִשְׂרָאֵל?

Using the Photograph

Direct your students to look at the photograph on page 55. Ask: What is printed above the telephone?

Pay-Phone — טֶלֶפוֹן מַטְבְּעוֹת

Students will not know the second Hebrew word ("coins"), but they can recognize טֶלֶפוֹן. Call on a student to read the caption.

Chapter 10 • בְּתֵל-אָבִיב

Introducing the Dialogue

Ask:

- If you were visiting Israel, why might you want to eat pizza? *(Answers may include: to eat something familiar, to eat something I know I like)*
- If you were visiting Israel, why might you want to eat falafel? *(Answers may include: to experience real Israeli food, the falafel in Israel is better than falafel in North America)*

Tell students that in our next dialogue we will listen in as the friends talk about what they want to eat, Israeli or familiar foods.

Using the Illustration

Divide the class into groups of 3–4 students. Challenge the groups to write a short story of at least ten sentences about the illustration on page 58. After five to ten minutes, call on a representative from each group to read the group's story to the class.

In Our Restaurant

Have the class brainstorm all the foods and drinks they can name in Hebrew. Write these words on the board. Divide the class into small groups and give each group a large sheet of construction paper on which they should create a menu in Hebrew that could be displayed in the window of a restaurant. Encourage students to illustrate the menu. For fun, students can make up prices and star ratings for their dishes. Invite students to come to the front of the room, to show the class the group's menu and to ask classmates:

מַה אַתָּה/אַתְּ רוֹצֶה/רוֹצָה לֶאֱכוֹל בַּמִסְעָדָה שֶׁלָנוּ?

מַה אַתָּה/אַתְּ רוֹצֶה/רוֹצָה לִשְׁתּוֹת בַּמִסְעָדָה שֶׁלָנוּ?

Falafel for All

Turn your classroom into a Tel Aviv falafel restaurant. Divide the class into groups and have some students prepare Israeli salad while others prepare falafel. Perhaps invite a few parents to help with this activity. Prepare falafel using a recipe, falafel mix, or frozen falafel. Recipes can be found in many cookbooks as well as on the Internet. Students can make their own sandwiches of pita, salad, falafel, and tehina.

Concentration

Using twelve index cards of one color, make four word cards with each of the following three pronouns: אַתְּ, אַתָּה, אַתֶּם. Using twelve index cards of another color, prepare the following word cards: אוֹכְלִים, אוֹהֲבִים, עוֹבְדִים, נוֹסְעִים, רוֹאֶה, יָפֶה, בָּא, חָבֵר, צְרִיכָה, יַלְדָה, רוֹצָה, גָּרָה. Or use words of your own choice. Place all the word cards face down. Divide the class into two teams, א and ב. Explain that the teams will try to pick a pronoun and a word that matches by gender and number, then build a sentence with those words (adding a third word that they know, if they choose), and correctly translate the sentence into English.

Teams take turns picking cards and making sentences. Award a team one point for a correct match, one point for a correct sentence, and one point for a correct translation. If the team earns all three points, remove the matching pair of cards. If the team fails to do any of these three tasks, place the cards back in their original positions and have the other team take a turn. Continue the game until all cards have been removed. The team with the most points wins.

Favorite Places to Eat

Draw three columns on the board and label them:

בַּבַּיִת – בְּמִסְעָדָה – בַּבַּיִת וְגַם בְּמִסְעָדָה

Invite a student to the front of the room, point to the choices on the board and ask the student:

אֵיפֹה אַתָּה/אַתְּ אוֹהֵב/אוֹהֶבֶת לֶאֱכוֹל?

The student must answer in a complete sentence.

Answers include:

אֲנִי אוֹהֵב/אוֹהֶבֶת לֶאֱכוֹל בַּבַּיִת.

אֲנִי אוֹהֵב/אוֹהֶבֶת לֶאֱכוֹל בְּמִסְעָדָה.

אֲנִי אוֹהֵב/אוֹהֶבֶת לֶאֱכוֹל בַּבַּיִת וְגַם בְּמִסְעָדָה.

That student then calls on another to ask where he or she likes to eat. The second student responds and then asks another student. Continue until all students have had a turn asking and answering.

Tel Aviv

Tell students that Tel Aviv is a very modern city located on the Mediterranean Sea. Ask:

- What would you expect to find in Tel Aviv? *(Answers may include: skyscrapers, museums, restaurants)* List students' responses on the board. If the students have missed any types of sites add those to the list. Be sure the list includes: beaches, theaters, a concert hall, museums, a university, the stock exchange, malls, and many kinds of restaurants and stores.
- What makes Tel Aviv different from a coastal city in North America? *(Answers may include: has many more synagogues; store signs, clothing labels, and menus are all in Hebrew; offers falafel and other Israeli foods)*

Explain that in Tel Aviv the shops and theaters have *mezuzot* on their doors. Tel Aviv even has a beach for observant Jews where the men and women do not swim together; instead, they swim on alternate days. If your students made a poster about Tel Aviv (see chapter 5), invite one of the creators to explain to the class what is depicted on the poster.

Using the Photograph

Direct the class to read aloud the caption below the photograph on page 60. Ask:

What is unusual about this photograph? *(A bride and groom are dressed in wedding garments and eating in a simple restaurant)* Invite students to make up short stories (in English) that tell about the events that preceded the photograph.

Chapter 11 • בַּת-מִצְוָה בִּירוּשָׁלַיִם

Introducing the Dialogue

Ask students questions about their bar and bat mitzvah, such as:

- What will you be learning/are you learning for your bar and bat mitzvah ceremony? *(Answers may include: to lead prayers, to chant Torah and/or Haftarah, the contents of the Torah portion in preparation for writing a sermon)*
- What do you think will be easiest and what will be most challenging for you to learn?
- What do you expect to be the most interesting part of your bar or bat mitzvah preparation?
- Will you and your family be traveling to Israel for your bar or bat mitzvah? If so, where will you have the ceremony and who will be there?

Explain that in this chapter we will join Maya for her bat mitzvah ceremony in Jerusalem and see what she has learned for her bat mitzvah.

Using the Illustration

Direct your students to look at the illustration on page 64. Invite one student to the front of the room to pretend to be Maya. Call on others to ask "Maya" questions that are related to the illustration and/or the dialogue for chapter 11.

Questions may include:

יֵשׁ לָךְ טַלִּית?
מָה אַתְּ קוֹרֵאת?
בֵּן בָּא לְבֵית-הַכְּנֶסֶת?

The student who is "Maya" should respond to all the questions.

Trope

Ask your students why we use commas, periods and exclamation marks when we write. *(Answers may include: without these marks we would not know when to pause or when a sentence ends, the marks help us to understand what we are reading)* Explain that trope is just like punctuation. It tells us when to pause, stop, and emphasize words in a sentence. Each trope mark has a name, and serves a particular function, such as a pause, stop, or connector.

Direct your students to open a siddur to the V'ahavta and point out the trope marks. If your students know how to chant the V'ahavta, explain that their chanting is based on the Torah trope. If your students do not know how to chant the V'ahavta, sing it for them, have them listen to a recording, or have the cantor sing it for the class.

If your students have begun to learn the blessing before the Haftarah reading, ask them to open to this blessing in their siddurim. Have the class sing the blessing together. Explain that the melody is based on the Haftarah trope. If any of your students have already begun learning their Torah or Haftarah readings, let them sing a few lines for their classmates.

Mazal Tov

Teach your students — or invite the cantor or music teacher to teach — the song סִימָן טוֹב וּמַזָּל טוֹב.

סִימָן טוֹב וּמַזָּל טוֹב, וּמַזָּל טוֹב וְסִימָן טוֹב (3x)
יְהֵא לָנוּ.
יְהֵא לָנוּ, יְהֵא לָנוּ, וּלְכָל יִשְׂרָאֵל. (3x)

Explain that this is often sung in synagogue after a special *aliyah* for a happy occasion such as a baby naming, wedding, bar mitzvah, or bat mitzvah.

Simon Says

Begin by writing לָקוּם and its English meaning (to get up) on the board. Tell students that you are going to play a game of שִׁמְעוֹן אוֹמֵר (Simon Says) and they should act out whatever שִׁמְעוֹן says they should do. Do a pre-game practice by saying each of the following infinitives and having students act out each one with you after you say it:

לְשַׂחֵק   לָשֶׁבֶת   לִקְנוֹת   לֶאֱכוֹל

לִשְׁתּוֹת   לָקוּם   לִרְאוֹת   לָלֶכֶת

To play: Begin by asking all students to stand (שִׁמְעוֹן אוֹמֵר לָקוּם). Then say and perform one of the above actions. If you say שִׁמְעוֹן אוֹמֵר before the action, then students should act it out. If you do not say שִׁמְעוֹן אוֹמֵר before the action, then anyone who imitates the action is out of the game.

The last student to remain in the game is the winner.

Family Talk

Write the following on the board:

בֶּן-דוֹד   סַבָּא   דוֹד   אִמָּא

בַּת-דוֹדָה   סַבְתָּא   דוֹדָה   אַבָּא

Invite a student to the front of the room to be interviewed. Call on other students to ask the interviewee about some of the members of his or her family. *Questions may include:*

- יֵשׁ לְךָ/לָךְ דוֹד? • אֵיפֹה הַדּוֹד גָּר?
- יֵשׁ לְךָ/לָךְ בֶּן-דוֹד? • אֵיפֹה בֶּן-דוֹד גָּר?
- אֵיפֹה אִמָּא שֶׁלְּךָ/שֶׁלָּךְ עוֹבֶדֶת?

Ask a few other students to come to the front of the room, one at a time, to be interviewed about their families. For fun, use a microphone as a prop.

Nice to Meet You

Call two students to the front of the room. Pretend to introduce them to one another. Direct them to reply נָעִים מְאֹד after being introduced. For example:

Teacher, pointing to Sarah, says: דָּוִד, זֹאת שָׂרָה

Sarah responds, saying: נָעִים מְאֹד

Teacher, pointing to David, says: שָׂרָה, זֶה דָּוִד

David responds, saying: נָעִים מְאֹד

Divide the class into groups of three or four students. Appoint one student in each group to make the introductions. The other students should respond using the phrase נָעִים מְאֹד.

Using the Photograph

Call on a student to read the caption below the photograph on page 67. Ask your students how they think this girl feels as she is reading Torah. Challenge them to say sentences in Hebrew that describe the photograph.

Sentences may include:

יַלְדָּה קוֹרֵאת בַּתּוֹרָה.

הַיַּלְדָּה אוֹהֶבֶת אֶת הַטַּלִּית.

הַיַּלְדָּה יָפָה.

Chapter 12 • בַּמִדְבָּר

Introducing the Dialogue

Inform your class that there are a few words in English that come from Hebrew words. Write גָּמָל on the board and have the class read the word out loud. Ask them to guess what animal got its English name from גָּמָל. *(camel)* Tell them that in this dialogue the travelers will be seeing many camels (גְּמַלִים) as they travel through the desert.

Using the Illustration

Direct your students to look at the illustration on page 70. Ask: מַה אַתֶּם רוֹאִים? Challenge your class to say ten sentences that describe the illustration. Draw a tally mark on the board for each new sentence a student says. Sample sentences are:

יֵשׁ גְּמַלִים בַּמִדְבָּר. דָּנִיאֵל צָרִיךְ לִשְׁתּוֹת מַיִם.
הַחֲבֵרִים נוֹסְעִים בַּמִדְבָּר.

Around the World

Play "Around the World" to review vocabulary from chapters 1–12. Have students sit in a semicircle. Assign a "world traveler" to stand behind the student at one end of the semicircle. Say any word in Hebrew from chapters 1–12. Only the "world traveler" and the student seated in front of him or her may say the word's English meaning. The first of the two students to answer correctly stands behind the next student in the semicircle; the student who did not answer is "out." If neither student answers correctly, provide the correct answer and present another word.

The goal is for the "world traveler" to travel completely around the "world" (the class) by correctly translating all of the words. If both students answer correctly at the same time, give another word.

My Journey in the Desert

Invite a student to come to the front of the room and to pretend that he or she is one of the travelers. Have that student tell the class in Hebrew about the journey through the desert.

Don't Leave Out a Word

Have students work with a partner. Direct each pair to create a conversation in which they use all the new vocabulary words from chapter 12. Invite several of the pairs to act out their conversation for the rest of the class.

Traveling Companions

Begin by telling the class with whom you like to travel. For example:

אֲנִי אוֹהֵב/אוֹהֶבֶת לִנְסוֹעַ עִם הַמִּשְׁפָּחָה.

Ask students with whom they like to travel:

עִם מִי אַתָּה/אַתְּ אוֹהֵב/אוֹהֶבֶת לִנְסוֹעַ?

Answers may include:

אֲנִי אוֹהֵב/אוֹהֶבֶת לִנְסוֹעַ עִם סַבְתָּא.
אֲנִי אוֹהֵב/אוֹהֶבֶת לִנְסוֹעַ עִם הַחֲבֵרִים.
אֲנִי אוֹהֵב/אוֹהֶבֶת לִנְסוֹעַ עִם גִּילָה.

Singular and Plural

Divide the class into two teams, א and ב. Challenge the teams to change sentences from singular to plural and vice versa by changing the pronouns and verbs. Sample sentences include:

- אֲנִי רוֹאֶה אוֹטוֹבּוּס. (אֲנַחְנוּ רוֹאִים אוֹטוֹבּוּס.)
- אֲנַחְנוּ גָּרִים בַּקִּבּוּץ. (אֲנִי גָּר בַּקִּבּוּץ.)
- אַתֶּם רוֹצִים לָשֶׁבֶת? (אַתָּה רוֹצֶה לָשֶׁבֶת?)

Have teams take turns saying new sentences. A team earns a point for each correct sentence. The team with the most points is the winner.

The Negev

Direct the class to read aloud the last line of the dialogue on page 71. Ask your students which two words indicate that the desert is large.

(נוֹסְעִים וְנוֹסְעִים)

Write נֶגֶב on the board and tell your students that the desert in Israel is called the Negev. Show where the Negev is located on a map of Israel. Explain that the Negev makes up 66%, over 6,700 square miles, of Israel.

Show your class photographs of the Negev.

Ask: Is the landscape of the Negev what you had imagined? Why is it important to turn desert land into fertile farmland?

To the South

Invite your cantor or music teacher to teach the song וּפָרַצְתָּ.

וּפָרַצְתָּ יָמָּה וָקֵדְמָה צָפֹנָה וָנֶגְבָּה

Ask students to think about the geography of Israel and to guess which word in the song means "to the south" (נֶגְבָּה — *the Negev is located in the southern part of Israel*). Tell your students that the Torah tells us that God said these words to Jacob in Genesis 28: "You shall spread out to the west and to the east, to the north and to the south."

Using the Photograph

Tell your students to look at the photograph on page 74. Ask:

מַה אַתֶּם רוֹאִים?

Answers include:

אֲנִי רוֹאָה גָּמָל.

אֲנִי רוֹאָה גָּמָל בִּירוּשָׁלַיִם.

אֲנִי רוֹאָה אֶת יְרוּשָׁלַיִם.

- Do you know why a camel would be in the city of Jerusalem rather than in the desert? *(There are places in Jerusalem where tourists can ride a camel.)*
- Have any of you ridden on a camel? If you have, please tell the class what it is like. (If none of the students have ridden a camel, describe how it is easy to get on the camel when it is crouched on the ground. The trickiest part is hanging on as the camel stands up — first the camel's back legs go up and then the front legs. You must be sure to hold on tightly. And don't forget to mention the distinctive camel smell!)
- How many of you would like to ride a camel?

Chapter 13 • בְּאֵילַת

Introducing the Dialogue

Ask:

- Have you ever seen brightly colored fish? Where?
- Have you ever been to a beach with a coral reef?
- Have you been to an aquarium that has an area that is a coral reef?

Direct your students to look at the photograph on page 81 to see a picture of a coral reef.

Using the Illustration

Explain that the class will now make up a story in Hebrew based on the illustration on pages 76 and 77. Go around the room having students take turns adding new sentences to the story.

Under the Sea

Have the class create a poster of an underwater scene in Eilat.

Prepare ahead of time: Short lists — one for each student — of two or three colors (for example: לָבָן, כָּחוֹל, צָהוֹב). Give each student (1) a 4" x 6" piece of white paper on which to draw a fish, (2) a list of colors, and (3) a 1" x 4" piece of white paper.

Direct students to draw and color a fish on the larger piece of paper, using the colors on their lists. Have yellow, green, red, black, and blue markers available. Ask students to write a Hebrew sentence on the small piece of paper that describes their fish, such as דָּג בְּצֶבַע לָבָן, כָּחוֹל, וְצָהוֹב.

Write דָּגִים בְּאֵילַת in the center of a blue sheet of poster board. Mount each of the fish illustrations with its description on the poster board.

Hot and Cold

Play a game of קַר וְחַם. Choose one student to go outside the classroom. Ask a second student to hide either a stuffed toy camel or a picture of a camel in the room. When the student reenters the room, that student, the "seeker," goes to a place that he or she believes the "camel" has been hidden and says הִנֵּה גָּמָל. The "hider" responds with either חַם, if the person is near the camel, or קַר, if the person is far from the camel. Allow the "seeker" five attempts to locate the camel. If the "seeker" finds the camel, with your class congratulate him or her by cheering *mazal tov*. After five attempts the "seeker" becomes the "hider." Choose a new student to be the next "seeker."

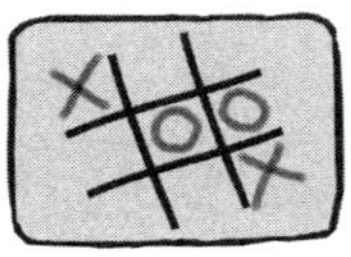

מַה הַמִּלָּה? — What's the Word?

Have a student choose a word from the chapter. The other students must guess what the word is, based on questions they ask. They can ask any question — in English — that will help them guess the word.

Suggested questions are:

- Is the word masculine or feminine?
- Is the word a person, place, or thing?
- How many letters are there in the word?

The class may ask as many questions as they like, but each student may guess only once. The student who guesses correctly receives a point and chooses the next word. The student with the most points at the end of ten rounds is the winner.

Is it Possible?

Divide the class into four groups. Challenge groups to compose as many questions as they can in three minutes that include the word אֶפְשָׁר followed by an infinitive. *Sentences may include:*

אֶפְשָׁר לִשְׁתּוֹת קָפֶה?
אֶפְשָׁר לִקְנוֹת בֶּגֶד-יָם פֹּה?
אֶפְשָׁר לִנְסוֹעַ לְחֵיפָה בָּאוֹטוֹבּוּס?

Call on a representative from each group to read its questions out loud. If another group has the identical question, both groups cross out that question. The group with the most correct questions wins.

Counting and Colors

Place ten sheets of colored construction paper in a row on the floor (two yellow, two red, two green, two white, two blue in random order). Walk alongside the row of papers and demonstrate counting and naming the color of the paper as you walk next to, not on, the papers. Challenge students to do the same. Be sure to change the order of the colors for each new student. For example, a student might call out:

אַחַת — כָּחוֹל, שְׁתַּיִם — יָרוֹק, שָׁלֹשׁ — אָדוֹם,
אַרְבַּע — לָבָן, חָמֵשׁ — אָדוֹם, שֵׁשׁ — צָהוֹב,
שֶׁבַע — צָהוֹב, שְׁמוֹנֶה — כָּחוֹל, תֵּשַׁע — לָבָן,
עֶשֶׂר — יָרוֹק.

Have the class join you in applauding each student that successfully completes the task.

Variation: Allow students to say just the names of the colors without the numbers.

Guardians of the Earth

According to Genesis 2:15, God puts Adam in the Garden of Eden to work it and to guard it. Just like Adam, we are obligated to take care of the world. We are all "*Shomrei Adamah*" (Guardians of the Earth) and "*Shomrei HaTeva*" (Guardians of Nature) who must protect and preserve the earth's natural resources and wonders. One of these wonders, Eilat's coral reef, is now threatened by dust and mud clouds that wash out to sea from shoreline construction and development projects. Sand that is brought in to create more beach front is not suitable for this region and harms the coral reef. In addition, there are inexperienced divers who break off bits of coral while they are diving. We, "*Shomrei Adamah*," need to protect the beautiful coral reefs of Eilat.

Using the Photograph

Have a student read the caption next to the photograph on page 81. Go around the room having each student take a turn saying a new sentence that includes either דָּג or דָּגִים.

Introducing the Dialogue

Ask: When do we say the שֶׁהֶחֱיָנוּ blessing? *(Answers may include: the first night of Ḥanukkah, when saying kiddush the first night of festivals, when using a lulav and etrog for the first time on Sukkot)*

If it has not yet been mentioned, inform students that we say שֶׁהֶחֱיָנוּ when doing something special for the first time. Explain that in this dialogue the friends and Maya's parents will say שֶׁהֶחֱיָנוּ when they visit a special place in Israel.

Using the Illustration

Begin a game of "Telephone" by whispering a sentence about the illustration on page 82 to a student. Have that student pass on the sentence to his or her neighbor. Continue until the sentence goes around the room. Have the last student say the sentence out loud and compare it to the original sentence.

Call on a student to make up another sentence about the illustration. Ask that student to whisper the sentence to you. If the sentence is correct then the student should whisper it to a fellow student, who will then begin to pass the sentence around the room. If the sentence is incorrect, quietly help the student correct the sentence and then have the student whisper the sentence to a classmate. Play several rounds of telephone, having different students make up sentences that describe the illustration.

What to Do?

Write the following infinitives on the board:

לֶאֱכוֹל לָלֶכֶת לִנְסוֹעַ לִקְנוֹת לִרְאוֹת לָשֶׁבֶת
לְשַׂחֵק לָשִׂים לִשְׁתּוֹת לַעֲלוֹת לָשִׁיר

Divide the class into three teams, א, ב, and ג. Say the English meaning of one of the infinitives.

Have the teams take turns saying the matching Hebrew word and making up a sentence with that word. A team earns one point for identifying the Hebrew word and two additional points for using it correctly in a sentence. You may use the same infinitive more than once during the game. The team with the most points wins.

Who? What? Where?

Ask students to work with a partner and to think of a מִי question, a מַה question, and an אֵיפֹה question about the dialogue. Invite one pair at a time to the front of the room and have them ask the class each of their questions. *Questions may include:*

מִי אוֹהֶבֶת לְשַׂחֵק בַּבּוֹץ?
מַה בֵּן אוֹהֵב לָשִׂים עַל הָאֹכֶל?
אֵיפֹה יַם-הַמֶּלַח?

Masada

Show your students photographs of Masada, which you can find in many books about Israel as well as on the Internet. Tell the history of Masada. For a short summary see *Welcome to Israel* (Behrman House), page 71. Inform students that many bar and bat mitzvah ceremonies take place at the ancient synagogue on Masada. Discuss why it would be special to become a bar or bat mitzvah on Masada.

שֶׁהֶחֱיָנוּ

Teach your students or invite your music teacher or cantor to teach your class to sing שֶׁהֶחֱיָנוּ.

בָּרוּךְ אַתָּה יְיָ אֱלֹהֵינוּ מֶלֶךְ הָעוֹלָם
שֶׁהֶחֱיָנוּ וְקִיְּמָנוּ וְהִגִּיעָנוּ לַזְּמַן הַזֶּה.

The Days of the Week

Ask:

- Which days of the week have you learned in Hebrew?
(list on the board: יוֹם שֵׁנִי, יוֹם רְבִיעִי, יוֹם חֲמִישִׁי)
- What numbers are related to the names of these days? (אַרְבַּע *[four] and* רְבִיעִי *both have the letters* רבע; חָמֵשׁ *[five] and* חֲמִישִׁי *both have the letters* חמש)

  Note: Since your students have only been taught שְׁתַּיִם and not שְׁנַיִם they may not see a connection between שְׁנַיִם and שֵׁנִי.
- If Thursday is the fifth day of the week, what is the seventh day? *(Saturday, Shabbat)*
Tell your students that the Hebrew names for the days of the week first appear in the story of creation in chapter 1 of Genesis.

List the names of the remaining days of the week and explain (or have students explain) how these names are related to numbers or other words students know. יוֹם רִאשׁוֹן, the head of the week, shares letters with רֹאשׁ (head); יוֹם שֵׁנִי shares letters with the masculine form for "two," שְׁנַיִם; יוֹם שְׁלִישִׁי is related to שָׁלֹשׁ; יוֹם שִׁשִּׁי is related to שֵׁשׁ. שַׁבָּת, meaning "rest," is not related to a number; rather it reminds us that God rested on the seventh day of creation.

New Word — New Sentence

Divide the class into two teams, א and ב. Begin by reading one sentence from the dialogue to א and challenge א to make a new sentence by replacing one word. ב must then make a new sentence replacing one word in the sentence said by א. For example: Begin with the dialogue sentence: בַּמִּדְבָּר יֵשׁ עוֹד יָם. א changes it to בְּיִשְׂרָאֵל יֵשׁ עוֹד יָם. Then ב changes it to בְּיִשְׂרָאֵל יֵשׁ עוֹד בֵּית-כְּנֶסֶת and א could change it to בְּיִשְׂרָאֵל אֵין עוֹד בֵּית-כְּנֶסֶת.

Tell students that the sentence needs to be grammatically correct, but it can be silly. Teams that successfully say a new correct sentence get a point. If a team fails to say a new correct sentence, read a new sentence from the dialogue and begin again. The team with the most points wins.

Using the Photograph

Call on a student to read the caption below the photograph on page 86. Ask:

מִי רוֹצֶה/רוֹצָה לְשַׂחֵק בַּבּוֹץ בְּיַם-הַמֶּלַח?

Call on a student and prompt him or her to say

אֲנִי רוֹצֶה/רוֹצָה לְשַׂחֵק בַּבּוֹץ בְּיַם-הַמֶּלַח.

Turn to another student and ask:

גַּם אַתָּה/אַתְּ?

Prompt that student to respond:

גַּם אֲנִי רוֹצֶה/רוֹצָה לְשַׂחֵק בַּבּוֹץ בְּיַם-הַמֶּלַח.

Ask several questions about the photograph. *Questions may include:*

הַבּוֹץ טוֹב?
חַם בְּיַם-הַמֶּלַח?
מִי רוֹצֶה/רוֹצָה לָצוּף בְּיַם-הַמֶּלַח?

Challenge students to ask their own questions in Hebrew.

Chapter 15 • לְהִתְרָאוֹת חֲבֵרִים!

Introducing the Dialogue

Ask:

- When you are on a trip, why do you buy souvenirs?
- Have you ever bought souvenirs for friends or relatives? What did you buy?
- In what kinds of places do you buy souvenirs?
- What makes the souvenir different from something you could buy at home?

Tell your students that in this chapter we will join the travelers as they buy souvenirs in a market.

Using the Illustration

Direct your students to look at the illustration on page 88 and ask:

- מַה בֵּן צָרִיךְ לִקְנוֹת? (בֵּן צָרִיךְ לִקְנוֹת כּוֹבַע.)
- בֵּן אוֹהֵב כּוֹבַע אָדוֹם? (לֹא, בֵּן אוֹהֵב כּוֹבַע יָרוֹק.)
- מַה אֶפְשָׁר לִקְנוֹת בַּשּׁוּק? (בַּשּׁוּק אֶפְשָׁר לִקְנוֹת כּוֹבַע וְגָמָל קָטָן.)

Divide class into groups of 3–4 students. Appoint one student in each group to be the shopkeeper and the other students to be the customers. Allow the groups five minutes to create a skit in which they are shopping at the שׁוּק. Invite groups to present their skits to the class..

Changing Gender and Number

Using any words from *Let's Talk!*, challenge students to change your sentence from feminine to masculine and vice versa. Next, challenge students to change the sentence from singular to plural and vice versa.

Bingo

Give each student a blank bingo board (5 squares across and 5 squares down). Have students fill in their bingo boards by writing in Hebrew words from the *milonim* of chapters 13–15.

With students' books open, say the English meaning of one of the *milon* words from chapters 13, 14, or 15 and have students place a marker (use small pieces of construction paper) over the Hebrew for the matching English word. The first student to make BINGO by placing five markers in a row horizontally, vertically or diagonally is the winner. Continue playing for second and third place winners

Find the Line

Invite a student to the front of the room. Show him or her a line from the dialogue. Ask the student to either pantomime or illustrate that line. Call on another student to guess which line was chosen from the dialogue. The student who guesses the correct line and reads the Hebrew correctly comes to the front to illustrate or pantomime a different line from the dialogue.

In a Big City

Have all students stand next to their seats. Each student must say a sentence about a big city that includes the words עִיר גְּדוֹלָה.

Sentences may include:

אֶפְשָׁר לֶאֱכוֹל בַּמִּסְעָדָה בְּעִיר גְּדוֹלָה.

אֶפְשָׁר לִקְנוֹת סַנְדָּלִים בְּעִיר גְּדוֹלָה.

אֶפְשָׁר לָשֶׁבֶת בְּבֵית-כְּנֶסֶת בְּעִיר גְּדוֹלָה.

If a student does not say a correct sentence, he or she sits down. The last student to remain standing wins.

When I Travel to Israel

Ask: What would you like to do on a trip to Israel? *Answers may include:*

אֲנִי רוֹצָה לָשֶׁבֶת עַל גָּמָל.
אֲנִי רוֹצָה לֶאֱכוֹל פָּלָפֶל בְּתֵל-אָבִיב.
אֲנִי רוֹצָה לִרְאוֹת קִבּוּץ.

Optional: Have each student write his or her response on a sentence strip. On a large poster board write:

אֲנַחְנוּ רוֹצִים לִנְסוֹעַ לְיִשְׂרָאֵל.

Mount all the sentences onto the poster board.

My Trip to Israel

Divide the class into four groups. Assign each group to be one of the friends from *Let's Talk!*: דִּינָה, בֵּן מַיָה, דָּנִיאֵל. Have each group prepare orally or write a paragraph in Hebrew, comprised of ten or more sentences, telling about his or her trip to Israel. Have a representative from each group read the account aloud to the class. Encourage students to read dramatically and, if they like, to bring in props.

Thanks

Ask: What does Daniel say to thank Maya's parents for the trip? (תּוֹדָה עַל הַטִּיּוּל הַיָּפֶה.)

Underline the phrase תּוֹדָה עַל. Divide the class into two teams, א and בּ. Say a noun in English for which students have learned the Hebrew in *Let's Talk!* *(Nouns may include: the clothing, the juice, the ball)* Team א must thank you for that thing. *Answers may include:*

תּוֹדָה עַל הַבְּגָדִים.
תּוֹדָה עַל הַמִּיץ.
תּוֹדָה עַל הַכַּדּוּר.

Alternate giving Team א and Team בּ nouns. Each team earns a point for a correct sentence. The team with the most points wins.

Things We Need

Have your students sit in a large circle. Have each student complete the sentence:

מָחָר אֲנִי נוֹסֵעַ/נוֹסַעַת לְיִשְׂרָאֵל וַאֲנִי צָרִיךְ/צְרִיכָה ________.

Before adding their own item (which must be a new item), students must repeat in order all of the items mentioned before their turn. For example:

רוּת צְרִיכָה כּוֹבַע, אִילָן צָרִיךְ סַנְדָּלִים.
מָחָר אֲנִי נוֹסֵעַ לְיִשְׂרָאֵל וַאֲנִי צָרִיךְ בֶּגֶד-יָם.

Continue until all students have had a turn. Allow them to help classmates who get stuck. This gets more challenging, and funnier, as you get farther around the circle.

Using the Photograph

Have the class read aloud the caption next to the photograph on page 90. Ask: Which color's letters are found in the word יְרָקוֹת? (יָרוֹק — *green*)

Why does it make sense that vegetables are called יְרָקוֹת? *(many vegetables are green)*

Look at this photograph of the שׁוּק as well as the illustration on page 88. How would you describe a שׁוּק? *(Answers may include: it is outdoors, there is a wide variety of items for sale, it has many small stands and stores)*

What might the men in the photograph be saying to each other in Hebrew? *Answers may include:*

אֶפְשָׁר לִקְנוֹת סָלָט?
אֲנִי רוֹצָה לִקְנוֹת יְרָקוֹת.
יֵשׁ הַרְבֵּה יְרָקוֹת.

Remembering Our Wish List

Remind students that before reading *Let's Talk!* the class had compiled a list of places they wanted to visit and things they wanted to do while in Israel. Review that list with the class to see if the characters visited any of the places or did any of the activities on the class's wish list.

Answers to Activities

Who Am I?

Answer each question by writing the correct Hebrew name in the space below the picture.

בֵּן מַיָה דָנִיאֵל דִינָה

1. מִי אַתְּ? אֲנִי **דִינָה**
2. מִי אַתָּה? אֲנִי **בֵּן**
3. אַתָּה **בֵּן**? לֹא, אֲנִי **דָנִיאֵל**
4. אַתְּ **דִינָה**? לֹא, אֲנִי **מַיָה**

Search and Circle

Circle the English meaning of each Hebrew word.

1. שָׁלוֹם	yes	(hello)	I
2. כֵּן	hello	no	(yes)
3. אַתָּה	who	(you (m))	you (f)
4. לֹא	I	(no)	yes
5. מִי	(who)	I	you (f)
6. אֲנִי	who	hello	(I)

6

Word Search

Write the English meaning next to each Hebrew word.

אֲנִי	**I**
מִי	**who**
אַתָּה	**you (m)**
אַתְּ	**you (f)**
לֹא	**no**

Now find and circle each of the Hebrew words in the grid on the right.

ה	א	ל
א	נ	מ
ת	י	מ
ה	ת	א

Make the Connection

Draw a line to connect each Hebrew word to its English meaning.

I	שָׁלוֹם
hello	כֵּן
who	אַתָּה
you (m)	לֹא
yes	מִי
no	אַתְּ
you (f)	אֲנִי

7

CHAPTER

1

Who Are You?

Work with a partner. Fill in the blank spaces below using your Hebrew name and your partner's Hebrew name.

You: אֲנִי ________. מִי אַתָּה/אַתְּ?

Your partner: אֲנִי ________.

You: שָׁלוֹם ________.

Your partner: שָׁלוֹם ________.

Picture Perfect

Draw a picture of yourself. Then write a Hebrew caption introducing yourself.

8

Pass the Pencil

Work in groups of three or more. One person reads the first line out loud, checks it off with a pencil, then passes the pencil to the next person. The second person reads the next line, checks it off, and so on. Repeat the activity until everyone has read all the lines.

- ☐ מִי אַתְּ?
- ☐ אֲנִי דִינָה.
- ☐ שָׁלוֹם דִינָה.
- ☐ מִי אַתָּה?
- ☐ אֲנִי בֵּן.
- ☐ שָׁלוֹם בֵּן.
- ☐ אַתָּה בֵּן?
- ☐ לֹא, אֲנִי דָנִיאֵל.
- ☐ שָׁלוֹם דָנִיאֵל.
- ☐ אַתְּ דִינָה?
- ☐ לֹא, אֲנִי מַיָה.
- ☐ שָׁלוֹם מַיָה.

Triple Riddle

Circle every third letter below. Write the circled letters in the blank spaces to find the answer to the following riddle:
Which Hebrew word has three different meanings?

א ג (ש) ד ת (ל) מ צ (ו) פ ר (ם)

ש ל ו ם

שָׁלוֹם
The three meanings are *hello*, *good-bye*, and *peace*.

9

Where Do They Come From?

Complete each sentence by writing the Hebrew name of the place where each person lives.

אֲנִי מִ __נְיוּ-יוֹרְק__.

אֲנִי מִ __טוֹרוֹנְטוֹ__.

אֲנִי מִ __מֶקְסִיקוֹ__.

אֲנִי מִ __לוֹס-אַנְגְ'לֶס__.

אֲנַחְנוּ מִ __נְיוּ-יוֹרְק__.

A Perfect Fit

Circle the correct form of the verb in each sentence.

1. אִמָּא: אֲנִי נוֹסֵעַ/(נוֹסַעַת) לְיִשְׂרָאֵל.
2. דִינָה: אֲנִי נוֹסֵעַ/(נוֹסַעַת) לְלוֹס-אַנְגְ'לֶס.
3. אַבָּא: גַּם אֲנִי (נוֹסֵעַ)/נוֹסַעַת לְלוֹס-אַנְגְ'לֶס.
4. בֵּן: אֲנִי (נוֹסֵעַ)/נוֹסַעַת לְקַנָדָה.
5. דָנִיאֵל: אֲנִי (נוֹסֵעַ)/נוֹסַעַת לְמֶקְסִיקוֹ.
6. מַיָה: גַּם אֲנִי נוֹסֵעַ/(נוֹסַעַת) לְמֶקְסִיקוֹ.

12

Have a Nice Trip!

Write the number of the airplane ticket next to its matching Hebrew.

__5__ מִקַּנָדָה לְיִשְׂרָאֵל

__4__ מִנְיוּ-יוֹרְק לְטוֹרוֹנְטוֹ

__2__ מִיִשְׂרָאֵל לְמֶקְסִיקוֹ

__3__ מִיִשְׂרָאֵל לְלוֹס-אַנְגְ'לֶס

__1__ מִנְיוּ-יוֹרְק לְלוֹס-אַנְגְ'לֶס

You're the Author!

Make up your own story by picking a word from the choices on each line.
Remember: The verb must match masculine or feminine words. Then read your story out loud.

1. שָׁלוֹם. אֲנִי מַיָה/דָנִיאֵל/בֵּן.
2. אֲנִי מִמֶּקְסִיקוֹ/מִנְיוּ-יוֹרְק/מִלוֹס-אַנְגְ'לֶס.
3. אֲנִי נוֹסֵעַ/נוֹסַעַת/נוֹסְעִים לְיִשְׂרָאֵל/לְקַנָדָה.
4. הִנֵּה אַבָּא/אִמָּא שֶׁלִּי.
5. גַּם אַבָּא שֶׁלִּי נוֹסֵעַ/נוֹסַעַת/נוֹסְעִים לְיִשְׂרָאֵל/לְקַנָדָה.
6. אִמָּא נוֹסַעַת? כֵּן/לֹא.
7. שָׁלוֹם מֶקְסִיקוֹ/נְיוּ-יוֹרְק/לוֹס-אַנְגְ לֶס.
8. אֲנַחְנוּ נוֹסְעִים לְיִשְׂרָאֵל/לְקַנָדָה.

13

CHAPTER 2

Jet Set

On the blank lines, write the English word that matches the Hebrew word above.
Choose from the following words:

you (m)
here is/are
hello
also
we
travel (m pl)

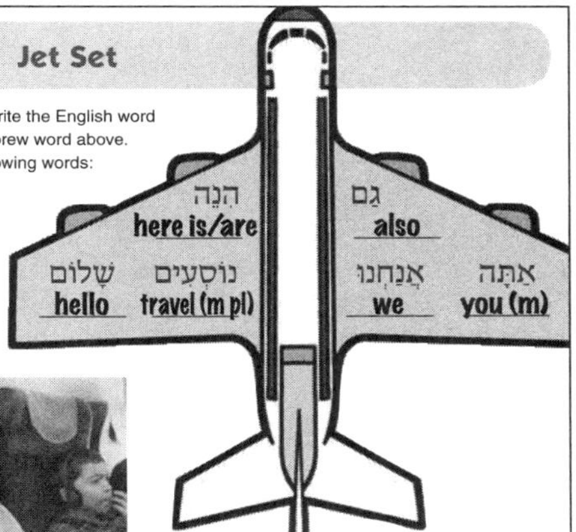

אֲנַחְנוּ נוֹסְעִים לְיִשְׂרָאֵל.

Yes or No?

Read the story on pages 10-11.
Then answer each question by writing כֵּן or לֹא.

1. דָנִיאֵל מִלוֹס-אַנְגְ'לֶס? __כֵּן__
2. בֵּן נוֹסֵעַ לְטוֹרוֹנְטוֹ? __לֹא__
3. מַיָה נוֹסַעַת לְיִשְׂרָאֵל? __כֵּן__
4. דִינָה מִנְיוּ-יוֹרְק? __לֹא__
5. אַבָּא וְאִמָּא נוֹסְעִים לְיִשְׂרָאֵל? __כֵּן__
6. מַיָה וְדִינָה נוֹסְעוֹת לְחֵיפָה? __לֹא__

14

Make the Connection

Connect each word or phrase in column א with a matching verb in column ב. The first example has been completed for you.

ב	א
נוֹסַעַת	דָנִיאֵל
נוֹסְעִים	אַתְּ
נוֹסְעוֹת	אֲנַחְנוּ
נוֹסֵעַ	מַיָה וְדִינָה
נוֹסְעִים	אַתָּה
נוֹסֵעַ	אַבָּא וְאִמָּא
נוֹסַעַת	מַיָה

(Lines drawn: דָנִיאֵל — נוֹסֵעַ; אַתְּ — נוֹסַעַת; אֲנַחְנוּ — נוֹסְעִים; מַיָה וְדִינָה — נוֹסְעוֹת; אַתָּה — נוֹסֵעַ; אַבָּא וְאִמָּא — נוֹסְעִים; מַיָה — נוֹסַעַת)

Tricky Travel

Write the Hebrew words from the list below on the blank lines next to the matching English.
Then complete the sentence at the bottom by copying the letters from the boxes.

הִנֵּה נוֹסַעַת גַּם נוֹסֵעַ שָׁלוֹם שֶׁלִּי

here is/are __ה נ ה__ (ה in box)

hello, good-bye, peace __ש ל ו ם__ (ו, ם in boxes)

travels (f) __נ ו ס ע ת__ (ס in box)

travels (m) __נ ו ס ע__ (ע in box)

my, mine __ש ל י__ (י in box)

also __ג ם__ (ם in box)

אַבָּא וְאִמָּא __נ ו ס ע י ם__ לְיִשְׂרָאֵל.

15

CHAPTER 3

Search and Circle

Circle the English meaning for each Hebrew word below.

because	(but)	on	1. אֲבָל
in	(what)	who	2. מָה
the	(big)	in	3. גָדוֹל
on	(head)	because	4. רֹאשׁ
(thank you)	but	hello	5. תּוֹדָה
hello	(now)	because	6. עַכְשָׁו

In the Bag

Draw a line connecting the Hebrew word to the matching item in the picture.

Artist at Work

Draw one picture of yourself to illustrate all three Hebrew sentences below.

יֵשׁ לִי תִּיק.
יֵשׁ לִי סַנְדָּלִים.
יֵשׁ לִי כּוֹבַע.

Now draw yourself again to illustrate the following sentences.

אֵין לִי כּוֹבַע.
אֵין לִי סַנְדָּלִים.
אֵין לִי תִּיק.

Crossword Puzzle

DOWN:
1. bag, backpack
2. big (m)
3. clothes
4. here is, here are

ACROSS:
5. who
6. kibbutz
7. sandals

			ת 1				
			י	מ 5			
ץ	ו	ב 3	ק 6				
		ג		ג 2			
		ד		ד			
		י		ו		ה 4	
		ם	י	ל	ד	נ	ס 7
						ה	

A Perfect Fit

Circle words of your choice to create your own sentences. (Hint: Pay attention to masculine and feminine words!) Read your sentences out loud.

1. אֲנִי/אַתָּה נוֹסֵעַ/נוֹסַעַת לְקִבּוּץ/לְקָנָדָה.
2. יֵשׁ לִי/אֵין לִי כּוֹבַע/סַנְדָּלִים בַּתִּיק/עַל הָרֹאשׁ.
3. יֵשׁ סַנְדָּלִים/בְּגָדִים בַּתִּיק שֶׁלִּי/שֶׁל אַבָּא.
4. דִּינָה/בֵּן וְאַבָּא נוֹסַעַת/נוֹסְעִים לְיִשְׂרָאֵל/לְנְיוּ-יוֹרְק.

Picture Match

Check the sentence that best describes each picture.

- [x] עַכְשָׁו יֵשׁ לִי כּוֹבַע.
- [ ] יֵשׁ כּוֹבַע גָּדוֹל בַּתִּיק.
- [ ] יֵשׁ לִי רֹאשׁ, אֲבָל אֵין לִי כּוֹבַע.

- [ ] הִנֵּה אִמָּא.
- [ ] נוֹסְעִים לְיִשְׂרָאֵל.
- [x] יֵשׁ סַנְדָּלִים בַּתִּיק.

- [ ] אַבָּא שֶׁל מַיָה נוֹסֵעַ לְקִבּוּץ.
- [ ] הַבְּגָדִים שֶׁל מַיָה בַּתִּיק.
- [x] יֵשׁ סַנְדָּלִים.

- [ ] אֵין לִי תִּיק.
- [ ] הִנֵּה אַבָּא שֶׁלִּי.
- [x] תּוֹדָה, עַכְשָׁו יֵשׁ לִי תִּיק.

Word Search

Read the Hebrew word in each box. Then find the word in the chain of letters and circle it. Write the meaning on the blank line.

but	בַּסְכּוֹעשֶׁתאֲבָל	אֲבָל
clothes	גתדבְּגָדִיםמבג	בְּגָדִים
travels	לגנוֹסֵעַתוֹעלת	נוֹסֵעַ
big	שִׁידָהמגָדוֹל	גָדוֹל
hello, good-bye, peace	בְּעַשׁשָׁלוֹםליד	שָׁלוֹם

Charades

Play charades with a classmate. Choose one of the sentences below (don't tell!) and act it out. Your classmate should describe in Hebrew what you are doing. Then switch roles.

1. יֵשׁ כּוֹבַע גָּדוֹל עַל הָרֹאשׁ.
2. מִי אַתָּה/מִי אַתְּ?
3. יֵשׁ בְּגָדִים, אֲבָל אֵין כּוֹבַע.
4. אֲנִי נוֹסֵעַ/אֲנִי נוֹסַעַת.
5. הַסַּנְדָּלִים בַּתִּיק.
6. אוֹי, הָרֹאשׁ שֶׁלִּי.

הִנֵּה בְּגָדִים. יֵשׁ תִּיק אֲבָל אֵין כּוֹבַע.

Bunch of Grapes

Write the number of the Hebrew words next to the matching English words.
You will have four Hebrew words left. Write a sentence with those four words.

1 בֵּן 2 קָפֶה 3 בְּבַקָּשָׁה 4 מִיץ

5 תֵּה 6 רוֹצֶה 7 עֲנָבִים 8 לֶאֱכוֹל 9 פֵּרוֹת

tea **5** juice **4** coffee **2** please **3** fruit **9**

Write your Hebrew sentence here: בֵּן רוֹצֶה לֶאֱכוֹל עֲנָבִים.

Now write it in English: **Ben wants to eat grapes.**

אֵין עֲנָבִים, אֵין בָּנָנָה.
יֵשׁ מִיץ? יֵשׁ פֵּרוֹת?

24

A Perfect Fit

Circle the correct form of the verb in each sentence.
Then read each sentence aloud, adding in the Hebrew word represented by the picture at the end of each sentence.

1. דִּינָה רוֹצָה/(רוֹצָה) לֶאֱכוֹל ___.
2. מַיָה וְדָנִיאֵל רוֹצָה/(רוֹצִים) לִשְׁתּוֹת ___.
3. בֵּן לֹא (רוֹצֶה)/רוֹצָה לִשְׁתּוֹת ___.
4. אִמָּא (נוֹסַעַת)/נוֹסְעִים עִם ___.
5. אַבָּא (רוֹצֶה)/רוֹצָה לֶאֱכוֹל ___.
6. מַיָה וְאִמָּא רוֹצָה/(רוֹצוֹת) לִשְׁתּוֹת ___.

Eat or Drink?

Write each of the words below in the לֶאֱכוֹל ("to eat") or לִשְׁתּוֹת ("to drink") column.

פֵּרוֹת מִיץ קָפֶה תֵּה עֲנָבִים מַיִם חָלָב סוּכָּר בָּנָנָה קוֹלָה

לֶאֱכוֹל	לִשְׁתּוֹת
פֵּרוֹת	מִיץ
עֲנָבִים	קָפֶה
סוּכָּר	תֵּה
בָּנָנָה	מַיִם
	חָלָב
	קוֹלָה

Circle the food and drink you like best.

25

CHAPTER 4

Make the Connection

Draw a line to connect the words that are opposites or pairs.

אֵין	כֵּן
בְּבַקָּשָׁה	יֵשׁ
לֶאֱכוֹל	תּוֹדָה
לֹא	לִשְׁתּוֹת

What's Happening?

Write the number of the Hebrew sentence that best decribes what you see in each picture.

1. יֵשׁ לִי בָּנָנָה.
2. מַיָה נוֹסַעַת לְיִשְׂרָאֵל.
3. אֵין לִי כּוֹבַע.
4. הִנֵּה מִיץ פֵּרוֹת.
5. יֵשׁ לִי כּוֹבַע.

4 **3**

1 **5** **2**

26

Tell Your Story

Fill in the blanks using the words below. Read your sentences to a classmate.

חָלָב סוּכָּר עֲנָבִים קָפֶה תֵּה מִיץ

1. יֵשׁ לִי קָפֶה (coffee), אֲבָל אֵין לִי סוּכָּר (sugar).
2. אַתְּ רוֹצָה לֶאֱכוֹל עֲנָבִים (grapes)?
3. לֹא, אֲנִי רוֹצָה לִשְׁתּוֹת מִיץ (juice).
4. אֲנִי רוֹצָה לִשְׁתּוֹת חָלָב (milk).
5. אַתָּה רוֹצֶה לִשְׁתּוֹת תֵּה (tea)?

Short Answers

Use the prefixes below to fill in the blanks in the sentences.

לְ__ מִ__ וְ__ הַ__ בְּ__

1. אִמָּא נוֹסַעַת מִטוֹרוֹנְטוֹ לְיִשְׂרָאֵל.
2. אֵין כּוֹבַע בַּתִּיק.
3. בֵּן וְדִינָה רוֹצִים לִשְׁתּוֹת מִיץ פֵּרוֹת.
4. דָּנִיאֵל נוֹסֵעַ מִנְיוּ-יוֹרְק לְמֶקְסִיקוֹ.
5. יֵשׁ בָּנָנָה וְסוּכָּר בַּתִּיק.

27

CHAPTER 5

Search and Circle

Circle the English meaning for each Hebrew word below.

1. אוֹטוֹבּוּס	Sunday	taxi	bus
2. לְהִתְרָאוֹת	see you again	hello	families
3. יוֹם רְבִיעִי	head	Wednesday	Monday
4. מוֹנִית	family	bus	taxi
5. מִשְׁפָּחָה	milk	family	we

Mix and Match Sentences

Use the words below to complete the sentences according to the story on pages 28-29.

בְּמוֹנִית   בְּחֵיפָה   בְּתֵל-אָבִיב   בָּאוֹטוֹבּוּס

1. בֵּן, הַמִּשְׁפָּחָה שֶׁלִּי ___בְּחֵיפָה___.
2. אֲנַחְנוּ נוֹסְעִים לִירוּשָׁלַיִם ___בְּמוֹנִית___.
3. אוֹי, בֵּן ___בָּאוֹטוֹבּוּס___.
4. שָׁלוֹם דָּנִיאֵל, לְהִתְרָאוֹת ___בְּתֵל-אָבִיב___.

יִשְׂרָאֵל!

Where Are They Going?

Based on the story on pages 28-29
draw a line from the person to the destination.
(Note: More than one person will be going to the same destination.)

אִמָּא	
בֵּן	חֵיפָה
דִּינָה	
מַיָה	יְרוּשָׁלַיִם
דָּנִיאֵל	
אַבָּא	קִבּוּץ

A Perfect Fit

Circle the correct form of the verb in each sentence. Then read each sentence aloud. (Hint: Pay attention to masculine and feminine words!)

1. דִּינָה רוֹאֶה/רוֹאָה אוֹטוֹבּוּס.
2. אַבָּא וְאִמָּא נוֹסֵעַ/נוֹסְעִים בְּמוֹנִית.
3. זֶה/זֹאת הַתִּיק שֶׁל בֵּן.
4. מַיָה, זֹאת הָאִמָּא שֶׁלְּךָ/שֶׁלָּךְ?
5. דָּנִיאֵל רוֹצֶה/רוֹצָה לֶאֱכוֹל פֵּרוֹת.
6. אַתָּה הַדּוֹד/הַדּוֹדָה שֶׁל בֵּן?

31

What Do You Say?

Write the number of the Hebrew word that matches the English word in each talk bubble.
Choose from the words below:

1. שָׁלוֹם 2. לְהִתְרָאוֹת 3. עַכְשָׁו
4. אֵיפֹה 5. יוֹם רְבִיעִי 6. בְּבַקָּשָׁה

hello 1
now 3
see you again 2
Wednesday 5
please 6
where (is) 4

Picture Match

Write the number of the Hebrew sentence that best describes each picture.

1. יֵשׁ לִי פֵּרוֹת.
2. הַמִּשְׁפָּחָה נוֹסַעַת בְּמוֹנִית.
3. לְהִתְרָאוֹת!
4. הִנֵּה כּוֹבַע גָּדוֹל.
5. בֵּן וְדִינָה נוֹסְעִים בָּאוֹטוֹבּוּס.

4

3

1

2

5

32

His and Hers

In each sentence below, circle either שֶׁלְּךָ ("your" for a boy) or שֶׁלָּךְ ("your" for a girl).

1. בֵּן, הִנֵּה הַתִּיק שֶׁלְּךָ/שֶׁלָּךְ.
2. דִּינָה, הַסַּנְדָּלִים שֶׁלְּךָ/שֶׁלָּךְ?
3. מַיָה, הִנֵּה אַבָּא שֶׁלְּךָ/שֶׁלָּךְ.
4. אַתָּה רוֹצֶה לִשְׁתּוֹת קוֹלָה? אֵיפֹה הַקּוֹלָה שֶׁלְּךָ/שֶׁלָּךְ?
5. דָּנִיאֵל, זֹאת הַדּוֹדָה שֶׁלְּךָ/שֶׁלָּךְ?

What's the Question?

Choose from the words below to complete the question for each answer.

מִי?   אֵיפֹה?   מָה?

1. ___מִי___ נוֹסֵעַ לִירוּשָׁלַיִם?
אַבָּא נוֹסֵעַ לִירוּשָׁלַיִם.
2. ___אֵיפֹה___ דִּינָה?
דִּינָה בַּקִּבּוּץ.
3. ___מָה___ יֵשׁ בַּתִּיק?
יֵשׁ בְּגָדִים בַּתִּיק.
4. ___מָה___ רוֹצֶה בֵּן לֶאֱכוֹל?
בֵּן רוֹצֶה לֶאֱכוֹל פֵּרוֹת.
5. ___אֵיפֹה___ הַסַּנְדָּלִים?
הַסַּנְדָּלִים בַּתִּיק.

33

Make the Connection

Connect each Hebrew word to its matching picture.

מוֹנִית

בֵּית-כְּנֶסֶת

פֵּרוֹת

אוֹטוֹבּוּס

חֲבֵרִים

Word Search

Find and circle each of the following Hebrew words in the grid below.
Then write the English meaning below each Hebrew word.

גָּרִים	חֲבֵרִים	גָּר, גָּרָה	קִבּוּץ	גַּן	קָטָן
live	friends, members	lives	kibbutz	garden	small

ת	ע	ח	ו
ץ	ו	ב	ק
ג	ק	ר	ג
ן	ט	י	ר
נ	ן	ם	ה
ם	י	ר	ג

36

His, Hers, or Ours

In each sentence below, write either שֶׁלְּךָ, שֶׁלָּךְ, or שֶׁלָּנוּ.

1. אֲנַחְנוּ גָּרִים בְּקִבּוּץ שֶׁלָּנוּ.
2. דִּינָה, הִנֵּה הַתִּיק שֶׁלָּךְ.
3. בֵּן, הַבְּגָדִים שֶׁלְּךָ בַּתִּיק.
4. דָּנִיאֵל בַּמּוֹנִית. דָּנִיאֵל: הַמּוֹנִית שֶׁלְּךָ.
5. אִמָּא, הַפֵּרוֹת שֶׁלָּךְ?
6. אַבָּא, אַתָּה רוֹצֶה לִשְׁתּוֹת מַיִם? הִנֵּה הַמַּיִם שֶׁלְּךָ.

יֶלֶד (boy) עוֹבֵד בְּקִבּוּץ.

37

CHAPTER 6

A Perfect Fit

Circle the correct word to complete each sentence.
Then read your sentences aloud.

1. אַתְּ חָבֵר/חֲבֵרָה שֶׁלִּי.
2. מַיָה וְאִמָּא גָּרִים/גָּרוֹת בְּנְיוּ-יוֹרְק.
3. דָּן נוֹסֵעַ/נוֹסַעַת מֵחֵיפָה לְתֵל-אָבִיב.
4. יֵשׁ הַרְבֵּה מִשְׁפָּחָה/מִשְׁפָּחוֹת בַּקִּבּוּץ.
5. אַבָּא עוֹבֵד/עוֹבֶדֶת בְּנְיוּ-יוֹרְק.
6. דָּנִיאֵל רוֹצֶה/רוֹצָה לֶאֱכוֹל בַּחֲדַר-הָאֹכֶל.

In the Dining Room

Complete the story by filling in the missing words below.

1. הַמִּשְׁפָּחָה (family) שֶׁלִּי רוֹצָה (wants) לֶאֱכוֹל בַּחֲדַר - אֹכֶל (dining room).
2. יֵשׁ הַרְבֵּה (many) מִשְׁפָּחוֹת בַּחֲדַר-הָאֹכֶל.
3. גַּם הַחֲבֵרִים (friends) שֶׁלִּי רוֹצִים לֶאֱכוֹל בַּחֲדַר-הָאֹכֶל.
4. אֲנִי לֹא רוֹצָה פֵּרוֹת (fruit).

38

Odd One Out

In each line, circle the word that does not belong.
Then draw a picture to illustrate the word you circled.

1. בָּנָנָה עֲנָבִים פְּרִי כּוֹבַע ________
2. אַבָּא אֲנִי אַתָּה אֲנַחְנוּ ________
3. כּוֹבַע סַנְדָּלִים מִיץ בְּגָדִים ________
4. נוֹסֵעַ נְיוּ-יוֹרְק נוֹסַעַת נוֹסְעִים ________
5. חָלָב קָפֶה מַיִם אוֹטוֹבּוּס ________
6. בֵּית-כְּנֶסֶת דּוֹד מִשְׁפָּחָה אִמָּא ________
7. בֵּית-סֵפֶר בֵּית-כְּנֶסֶת חֲדַר-הָאֹכֶל מוֹנִית ________
8. שָׁלוֹם! גַּן לְהִתְרָאוֹת! תּוֹדָה! ________

39

In the Basket!

In each basket, write the English word(s) that match(es) the Hebrew word(s) on the basketball. Choose from the words on the scoreboard.

to play ball
nice, pretty room
to put okay, all right
mountain basketball

- הַר — mountain
- כַּדּוּרְסַל — basketball
- בְּסֵדֶר — okay, all right
- לָשִׂים — to put
- כַּדּוּר — ball
- לְשַׂחֵק — to play
- יָפֶה/יָפָה — nice, pretty
- חֶדֶר — room

A Perfect Fit

Circle the correct form of the verb in each sentence.
Then read your sentences aloud.

1. דָנִיאֵל (אוֹהֵב)/אוֹהֶבֶת לְשַׂחֵק כַּדּוּרֶגֶל.
2. דִינָה רוֹצֶה/(רוֹצָה) לֶאֱכוֹל בַּנָנָה.
3. הַיְלָדִים גָר/גָרָה/(גָרִים) בְּתֵל-אָבִיב.
4. מַיָה וְדִינָה אוֹהֲבִים/(אוֹהֲבוֹת) לְשַׂחֵק כַּדּוּרְסַל.

42

What's the Question?

Write the number of each answer in the space next to the corresponding question.

Q.	A.
שָׁלוֹם, מַה שְׁלוֹמְךָ? __3__	① דִינָה בַּחֶדֶר.
מִי בַּבַּיִת? __5__	② לֹא, תּוֹדָה. אֲנִי רוֹצָה לְשַׂחֵק כַּדּוּרְסַל.
אֵיפֹה דִינָה? __1__	③ טוֹב, תּוֹדָה.
אַתָּה רוֹצֶה לֶאֱכוֹל? __4__	④ כֵּן, תּוֹדָה. אֲנִי רוֹצֶה לֶאֱכוֹל עֲנָבִים.
אַתְּ רוֹצָה לְשַׂחֵק כַּדּוּרֶגֶל? __2__	⑤ בֵּן בַּבַּיִת.

הַבַּיִת עַל הַר הַכַּרְמֶל בְּחֵיפָה.

43

CHAPTER 7

Picture Match

Put a ✔ next to the sentence if the picture matches the Hebrew.
Put an ✘ if the picture does not match the Hebrew.

1. ✘ הַכַּדּוּר בַּתִּיק.
2. ✔ הַיַּלְדָּה אוֹהֶבֶת לֶאֱכוֹל.
3. ✔ הִנֵּה הַתִּיק שֶׁלִּי.
4. ✔ הַסַּנְדָּלִים בַּתִּיק.

Pass the Pencil

Work in groups of three or more. One person reads the first line out loud, checks it off with a pencil, then passes the pencil to the next person. The second person reads the next line, checks it off, and so on. Repeat the activity until everyone has read all the lines.

- ☐ שָׁלוֹם מַיָה, מַה שְׁלוֹמֵךְ?
- ☐ בְּסֵדֶר. מַה שְׁלוֹמְךָ?
- ☐ הַבַּיִת בִּירוּשָׁלַיִם.
- ☐ הַיְלָדִים אוֹהֲבִים לְשַׂחֵק כַּדּוּרֶגֶל.
- ☐ יֵשׁ כּוֹבַע גָדוֹל בַּתִּיק.
- ☐ בְּבַקָשָׁה לָשִׂים אֶת הַבְּגָדִים בַּחֶדֶר.
- ☐ עַכְשָׁו אֲנִי נוֹסַעַת לַקִּבּוּץ.
- ☐ יֵשׁ לִי קָפֶה, אֲבָל אֵין לִי חָלָב.

44

Tell Your Story

Write one or two sentences describing what you see in each picture.

45

Word Search

Read the Hebrew word in each box. Find the word in the chain of letters and circle it. Then write its meaning in the space.

Meaning	Chain of letters	Word
today	אֲעפּטלְהַיּוֹם	הַיּוֹם
store	נוֹחֲנוּתגד	חֲנוּת
prayer	קְתְּפִילָּהעֵז	תְּפִילָּה
tomorrow	אִיחֲמָחָרלוֹן	מָחָר
flag	טוּסדֶּגֶלאוֹר	דֶּגֶל
good	חלוֹטוֹבדן	טוֹב

Make the Connection

Draw a line from each Hebrew word to its English meaning.

skullcaps	חֲנוּת
to go, to walk	לִקְנוֹת
color	לָלֶכֶת
store	צֶבַע
to buy	כִּפּוֹת

A Perfect Fit

Circle the correct form of the word to complete each sentence. Then read your sentences aloud.

1. אִמָא וְאַבָּא רוֹאִים/רוֹאוֹת אֶת הַכֹּתֶל.
2. מַיָה רוֹצֶה/רוֹצָה לָשִׂים סַנְדָּלִים בַּתִּיק.
3. בֵּן, מַה שְׁלוֹמֵךְ/שְׁלוֹמְךָ?
4. הַיּוֹם דִּינָה צָרִיךְ/צְרִיכָה לָלֶכֶת לַחֲנוּת.
5. דָּן אוֹהֵב/אוֹהֶבֶת לְשַׂחֵק כַּדּוּרְסַל עִם מַיָה.
6. אֲנַחְנוּ גָּר/גָּרָה/גָּרִים בְּחֵיפָה.
7. כָּל הַחֲבֵרִים עוֹבֵד/עוֹבֶדֶת/עוֹבְדִים.
8. דִּינָה וְאִמָא נוֹסַעַת/נוֹסְעוֹת לִירוּשָׁלַיִם בְּמוֹנִית.

Make the Connection

Draw a line to connect the words that are opposites or pairs.

אֵין	כֵּן
תּוֹדָה	יֵשׁ
לָבָן	דּוֹד
לֶאֱכוֹל	בְּבַקָּשָׁה
אַבָּא	כָּחוֹל
מָחָר	אִמָא
לֹא	לִשְׁתּוֹת
דּוֹדָה	הַיּוֹם

CHAPTER 8

What's in the Store?

Draw a line from each Hebrew word or phrase to its matching picture.

כִּפָּה
כּוֹס קִדּוּשׁ
מְזוּזָה
טַלִּית
דֶּגֶל

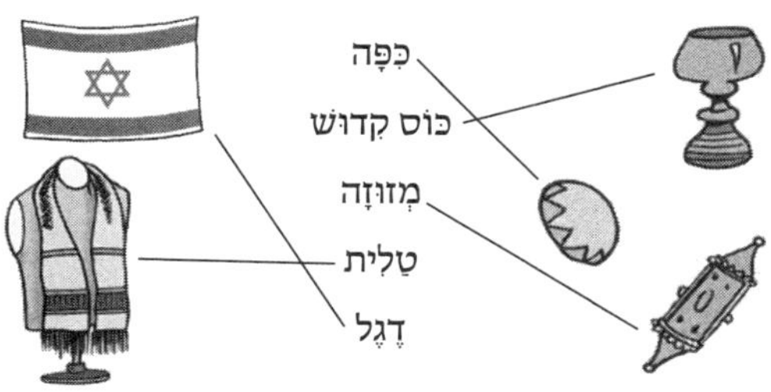

Plan Your Trip

You're going to visit Israel. Plan your trip!
Write the places you would like to see in the order you would like to see them.

תֵּל-אָבִיב חֵיפָה יְרוּשָׁלַיִם קִבּוּץ

Then draw a line to connect the place to the matching activity.

1. ____________ לִקְנוֹת כּוֹבַע בַּחֲנוּת
2. ____________ לִרְאוֹת אֶת הַר הַכַּרְמֶל
3. ____________ לֶאֱכוֹל בַּחֲדַר-הָאֹכֶל
4. ____________ לִרְאוֹת אֶת הַכֹּתֶל

Word Store

Complete the sentences below by filling in the missing words.

מָחָר הַטַּלִּית לָלֶכֶת הַכֹּתֶל לָשִׂים לִרְאוֹת

1. מַיָה, אַתְּ רוֹצָה __לָלֶכֶת__ לִרְאוֹת אֶת הַכֹּתֶל?
2. אִמָא, אַבָּא, אֲנִי רוֹאָה אֶת __הַכֹּתֶל__.
3. אֲנִי רוֹצָה __לָשִׂים__ תְּפִילָּה בַּכֹּתֶל.
4. __מָחָר__ אֲנַחְנוּ נוֹסְעִים __לִרְאוֹת__ אֶת הַכֹּתֶל.
5. מַיָה וְאִמָא אוֹהֲבוֹת אֶת __הַטַּלִּית__.

בַּחֲנוּת יֵשׁ חֲנוּכִּיָה.
יֵשׁ טַלִּית? יֵשׁ מְזוּזָה?

Answer the Telephone!

Write the number of each English word next to the telephone with the matching Hebrew word.

(1) good (m) (2) Wednesday
(3) at ___ o'clock
(4) next to (5) number
(6) good (f) (7) hour

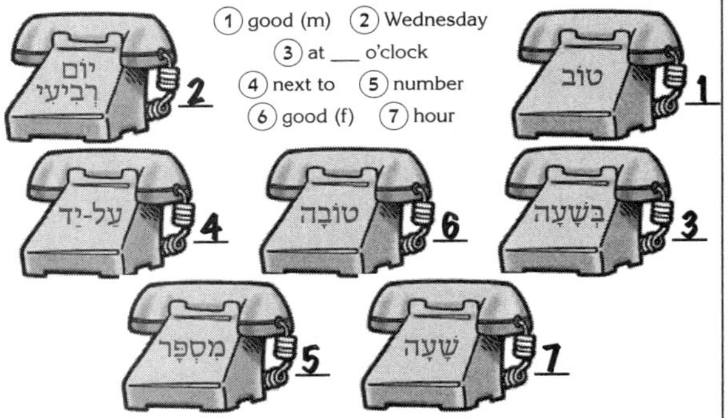

You're Invited

Read the invitation.
Then fill out the response card.

בַּר-מִצְוָה שֶׁל בֵּן
בְּיוֹם שַׁבָּת
בְּשָׁעָה עֶשֶׂר
בְּבֵית-הַכְּנֶסֶת

Can you attend? Circle one: כֵּן/לֹא

To reply by telephone, write the following numbers in the spaces below.
(Hint: Read the Hebrew from the right, but write the numbers from the left.)

שֶׁבַע, שֵׁשׁ, שְׁתַּיִם, אַרְבַּע, אַחַת, אֶפֶס, תֵּשַׁע

7 6 2 - 4 1 0 9

Grand Prix Race

Play in pairs. The player whose birthday is closest to today decides who goes first. The first player reads the number out loud in Hebrew beginning at "Start." If that player forgets a number, it's the other player's turn. The first one to reach the finish line wins!

מַה מִסְפַּר הַטֶּלֶפוֹן
שֶׁלְּךָ/שֶׁלָּךְ?

CHAPTER 9

What's Your Order?

The friends order food by number.
What does each friend order? Write the answer in English on each plate.

1. פִּיצָה
2. פָלָפֶל
3. בּוּרִיטוֹ
4. חָלָב
5. מִיץ
6. קוֹלָה
7. מַיִם
8. עֲנָבִים

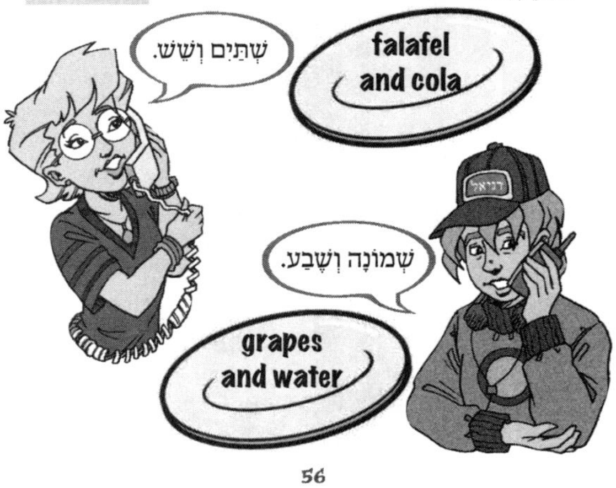

How Many?

Write the Hebrew word for each number.

1. (8) שְׁמוֹנֶה יְלָדוֹת בַּגַּן.
2. דָּנִיאֵל רוֹצֶה לִקְנוֹת (5) חָמֵשׁ כִּפּוֹת.
3. יֵשׁ לִי אִמָּא (1) אַחַת.
4. (4) אַרְבַּע מִשְׁפָּחוֹת בָּאוֹטוֹבּוּס.

Shortcut

Go from Jerusalem to Tel Aviv in just five steps. Start at the top row and trace a shortcut by finding the Hebrew for the five English words below. Move down one space at a time.

Shortcut: 1. ten 2. next to 3. okay 4. prayers 5. tomorrow

יְרוּשָׁלַיִם

אַחֵר	שָׁעָה	עֶשֶׂר	מִסְפָּר	טוֹב
הִנֵּה	אֲבָל	רֹאשׁ	עַל-יַד	כּוֹבַע
לָשִׂים	קָטָן	בְּסֵדֶר	יָפֶה	תּוֹדָה
שֵׁשׁ	כָּל	תְּפִלּוֹת	עוֹבְדִים	הַר
שְׁמוֹנֶה	מָחָר	חֲנוּת	דֶּגֶל	אֶפֶס

תֵּל-אָבִיב

Now create your own shortcut for a classmate.

A Perfect Fit

Circle the correct form of the verb to complete each sentence.
Then read your sentences aloud.

1. דִּינָה בָּא/**בָּאָה**/לַמִּסְעָדָה.
2. הַדּוֹדָה וְאִמָּא בָּאָה/**בָּאוֹת**/לַבַּיִת.
3. דָּוִד וְדוֹדָה/**בָּאִים**/בָּאוֹת לְבֵית-הַכְּנֶסֶת.
4. דָּנִיאֵל/**בָּא**/בָּאָה/בָּאִים לַקִּבּוּץ.
5. בֵּן/**בָּא**/בָּאָה לְתֵל-אָבִיב.

אוֹכְלִים וְשׁוֹתִים בְּמִסְעָדָה.

Yes or No?

Read each of the following sentences and based on the story decide whether it is true or false. Circle the letter in the correct column, כֵּן or לֹא.

כֵּן	לֹא	
ב	ח	1. הַחֲבֵרִים בַּמִּסְעָדָה.
ת	ט	2. בְּיִשְׂרָאֵל לֹא אוֹכְלִים פִּלְפֵּל.
מ	ל	3. דִּינָה רוֹצָה פִּלְפֵּל עִם סָלָט.
צ	פ	4. דָּנִיאֵל רוֹצֶה לִשְׁתּוֹת חָלָב.
ו	ק	5. דָּנִיאֵל בָּא לִירוּשָׁלַיִם.
ה	א	6. בְּתֵל-אָבִיב אֵין אוֹטוֹבּוּס לִירוּשָׁלַיִם.

Copy each circled letter in the numbered space below to find a mystery phrase.

מָחָר בַּ ת-הַ מִ צְ וָ ה שֶׁל מַיָּה.

5 5 4 3 2 1

Picture Perfect

Choose one of the sentences above and draw it in the frame.

CHAPTER

10

Make the Connection

Draw a line from each Hebrew word to its English meaning.

food	אַתֶּם
restaurant	אֹכֶל
cakes	יוֹם חֲמִישִׁי
you (pl)	עוּגוֹת
Thursday	מִסְעָדָה

A Perfect Fit

Fill in one of the following words to complete each sentence:

אַתְּ אַתָּה אַתֶּם

1. __אַתֶּם__ נוֹסְעִים מִנְיוּ-יוֹרְק לְתֵל-אָבִיב.
2. __אַתְּ__ רוֹצָה לִשְׁתּוֹת קָפֶה עִם חָלָב?
3. __אַתָּה__ רוֹאֶה כַּדּוּר?
4. __אַתָּה__ גָּר בְּחֵיפָה.
5. __אַתֶּם__ עוֹבְדִים בַּקִּבּוּץ.
6. __אַתְּ__ אוֹהֶבֶת לְשַׂחֵק כַּדּוּרְסַל.

Dial It Up

Choose one of the characters below and create your own Hebrew dialogue for him or her.
(Remember: Pay attention to masculine and feminine words.)
You can write key words from your dialogue on the blank lines.
Then share your dialogue with a classmate.

Search and Circle

Circle the English meaning for each Hebrew word.

congratulations	to sit	**pleased to meet you**	1. נָעִים מְאֹד
pleased to meet you	sing	**how are you (pl)**	2. מַה שְּׁלוֹמְכֶם
read (pl)	**congratulations**	cousin	3. מַזָּל טוֹב
lives (m/f)	**sings (m/f)**	six	4. שָׁר/שָׁרָה
grandfather	**grandmother**	cousin	5. סַבְתָּא
sing (pl)	how are you (pl)	**to sit**	6. לָשֶׁבֶת
aunt	**cousin (f)**	bat mitzvah	7. בַּת-דּוֹדָה
reads (m/f)	sings (m/f)	to buy	8. קוֹרֵא/קוֹרֵאת

Make the Connection

Draw a line from the statement or question on the right to the matching response on the left.

לְהִתְרָאוֹת!	זֶה אַבָּא וְזֹאת אִמָּא שֶׁלִּי.
תּוֹדָה.	אַתְּ רוֹצָה לֶאֱכוֹל?
טוֹב, תּוֹדָה.	הִנֵּה הָאוֹטוֹבּוּס!
נָעִים מְאֹד.	מַזָּל טוֹב!
כֵּן, אֲנִי רוֹצָה פֵּרוֹת בְּבַקָּשָׁה.	מַה שְּׁלוֹמֵךְ?

66

A Perfect Fit

Circle the correct form of the verb to complete each sentence. Then read your sentences aloud.

1. הַיְלָדִים בָּא/בָּאָה/**בָּאִים** לַמִּסְעָדָה.
2. בֵּן **קוֹרֵא**/קוֹרֵאת/קוֹרְאִים תְּפִילּוֹת.
3. אִמָּא צָרִיךְ/**צְרִיכָה** לָשֶׁבֶת.
4. סַבָּא וְסַבְתָּא **גָּרִים**/גָּרוֹת בְּבַיִת יָפֶה.
5. מַיָה וְאִמָּא שָׁרִים/**שָׁרוֹת** "אֲדוֹן עוֹלָם".

בַּת-מִצְוָה קוֹרֵאת בַּתּוֹרָה.

67

CHAPTER 11

What's the Question?

Copy the sentence that answers each question. (Hint: The number of the sentence is written in Hebrew at the end of each question!)

אֵיפֹה הַחֲבֵרִים? (חָמֵשׁ) הַחֲבֵרִים בְּבֵית-הַכְּנֶסֶת.

מִי גָּרָה בְּיִשְׂרָאֵל? (שָׁלֹשׁ) הַמִּשְׁפָּחָה שֶׁל מַיָה גָּרָה בְּיִשְׂרָאֵל.

מָה רוֹצֶה דָּנִיאֵל? (שְׁתַּיִם) דָּנִיאֵל רוֹצֶה טַלִּית.

יֵשׁ לְךָ כַּדּוּר? (אַחַת) לֹא, אֵין לִי כַּדּוּר.

מִי רוֹצֶה לֶאֱכוֹל? (אַרְבַּע) בֵּן רוֹצֶה לֶאֱכוֹל.

1. לֹא, אֵין לִי כַּדּוּר.
2. דָּנִיאֵל רוֹצֶה טַלִּית.
3. הַמִּשְׁפָּחָה שֶׁל מַיָה גָּרָה בְּיִשְׂרָאֵל.
4. בֵּן רוֹצֶה לֶאֱכוֹל.
5. הַחֲבֵרִים בְּבֵית-הַכְּנֶסֶת.

68

His and Hers

Connect each noun to its matching verb and write the English meaning of the verb on the blank line. Choose from the words below. The first example has been completed for you.

sings reads comes needs likes

דָּנִיאֵל — שָׁר; שָׂרָה — מַיָה: sings

דִּינָה — אוֹהֶבֶת; בֵּן — אוֹהֵב: likes

בֶּן-דּוֹד — קוֹרֵא; קוֹרֵאת — בַּת-דּוֹדָה: reads

סַבְתָּא — צְרִיכָה; צָרִיךְ — סַבָּא: needs

יֶלֶד — בָּא; בָּאָה — יַלְדָּה: comes

69

Enjoy the Ride

Write the number of the Hebrew below the matching English word on each bus.

(1) מִדְבָּר (2) טִיּוּל (3) מָקוֹם (4) גָּמָל
(5) כֵּיף (6) בֶּגֶד-יָם (7) חַם (8) לִנְסוֹעַ

A Perfect Fit

Circle the correct form of the verb in each sentence.

1. בֵּן רוֹצֶה נוֹסֵעַ/(לִנְסוֹעַ)/לַמִּסְעָדָה בִּמְכוֹנִית.
2. הַמִּשְׁפָּחָה רוֹצָה נוֹסַעַ/(לִנְסוֹעַ)/לַקִּבּוּץ.
3. מָיָה וְאִמָּא נוֹסַעַת/נוֹסְעִים/(נוֹסְעוֹת)/לִירוּשָׁלַיִם.
4. אֲנַחְנוּ (נוֹסְעִים)/לִנְסוֹעַ לְאֵילַת.

Camel Ride

Write the English word that matches the Hebrew word on each camel.
Choose from the following English words:

place, space very with fun hot

You will have five Hebrew words left over.
Write a sentence with those five words.

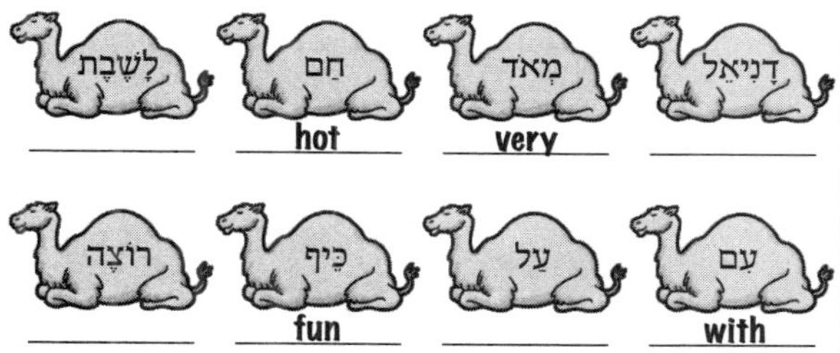

דָּנִיאֵל רוֹצֶה לָשֶׁבֶת עַל גָּמָל.

CHAPTER 12

Crossword Puzzle

Write the plural of each clue word in the spaces on the puzzle.

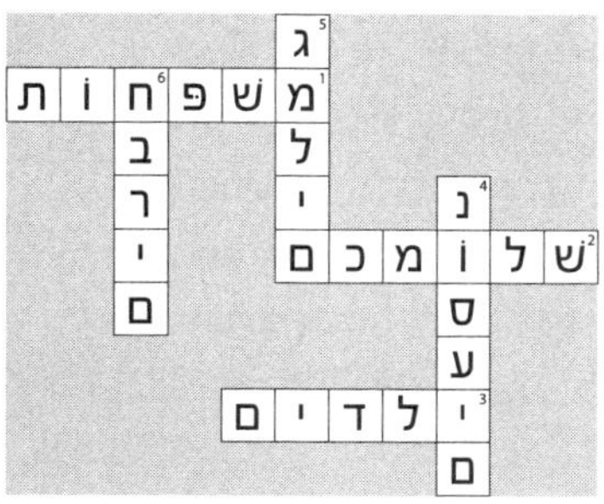

ACROSS:
1. מִשְׁפָּחָה
2. (מָה) שְׁלוֹמְךָ
3. יֶלֶד

DOWN:
4. נוֹסֵעַ
5. גָּמָל
6. חָבֵר

אַתָּה רוֹצֶה לָשֶׁבֶת עַל גָּמָל?
אַתְּ רוֹצָה לָשֶׁבֶת עַל גָּמָל?

What's Missing?

Write the Hebrew word(s) from the list below to complete each sentence.

בֶּגֶד-יָם לְהִתְרָאוֹת גָּמָל מָקוֹם כּוֹבַע

See you tomorrow at nine o'clock.	1. לְהִתְרָאוֹת מָחָר בְּשָׁעָה תֵּשַׁע.
I need a swim suit.	2. אֲנִי צְרִיכָה בֶּגֶד - יָם.
I see a camel.	3. אֲנִי רוֹאֶה גָּמָל.
There is a lot of space on the bus.	4. יֵשׁ הַרְבֵּה מָקוֹם בָּאוֹטוֹבּוּס.
I don't have a hat.	5. אֵין לִי כּוֹבַע.

It Adds Up!

Add or subtract the numbers. Write the answers in number form in the spaces.

שְׁמוֹנֶה + אַחַת = 9
שֶׁבַע + אֶפֶס = 7
שְׁתַּיִם + אַרְבַּע = 6
תֵּשַׁע - שָׁלֹשׁ + שְׁתַּיִם = 8
שֵׁשׁ - אַחַת = 5
חָמֵשׁ + חָמֵשׁ = 10

CHAPTER

13

Go Fishing!

On each boat, write the Hebrew word that matches the English word on the wave. Choose from the following words:

יָם דָגִים קַר

אֶפְשָׁר סִירָה

Word Families

On each line, cross out the verb that doesn't belong.

1. נוֹסֵעַ לִנְסוֹעַ נוֹסְעִים ~~לָשֶׁבֶת~~
2. שָׁר שָׁרָה ~~לִשְׁתּוֹת~~ שָׁרוֹת
3. קוֹרֵאת ~~לִקְנוֹת~~ קוֹרֵא קוֹרְאִים
4. גָר גָרִים ~~לִבְנוֹת~~ גָרָה
5. בָּא ~~לֶאֱכֹל~~ בָּאוֹת בָּאִים

Choose one verb you crossed out and give its English meaning.

Verb:________________ English meaning:________________

78

What Color?

Write the color of each fish in the blank space below it. Choose from the colors below:

יָרוֹק צָהוֹב כָּחוֹל אָדוֹם לָבָן

דָג לָבָן דָג יָרוֹק דָג כָּחוֹל דָג צָהוֹב דָג אָדוֹם

Rebus and Write

Write the correct Hebrew word in the space next to each picture. Choose from the words below.

דָג סִירָה דֶגֶל גָמָל כַּדּוּר

בֵּן: אֲנִי רוֹאֶה ___דָג___ בַּיָם.

מַיָה: זֶה לֹא ___דָג___, זֶה ___כַּדּוּר___.

בֵּן: אַתְּ רוֹאָה ___כַּדּוּר___ בְּצֶבַע יָרוֹק?

מַיָה: לֹא, אֲנִי רוֹאָה ___סִירָה___ בְּצֶבַע צָהוֹב.

בֵּן: מַה? אֵין ___סִירָה___.

אֲנִי רוֹאֶה ___דֶגֶל___ בְּצֶבַע כָּחוֹל וְלָבָן.

אַתְּ רוֹאָה ___גָמָל___?

מַיָה: לֹא, אֲנִי לֹא רוֹאָה ___גָמָל___.

בֵּן: טוֹב! גַם אֲנִי לֹא רוֹאֶה ___גָמָל___!

79

Opposites Attract

Draw a line to connect each word on the right to its opposite on the left.

חַם	גָדוֹל
יַלְדָה	לֹא
קָטָן	בַּת-דוֹדָה
כֵּן	קַר
בֶּן-דוֹד	יֶלֶד

At the Dock

Unscramble the words below to write a sentence.

דָגִים לִרְאוֹת רוֹצִים הַחֲבֵרִים לָלֶכֶת לַיָם

הַחֲבֵרִים רוֹצִים לָלֶכֶת לַיָם לִרְאוֹת דָגִים.

Secret Sail

Cross out every second letter in each row on the boat to discover the Hebrew words that match the English below.

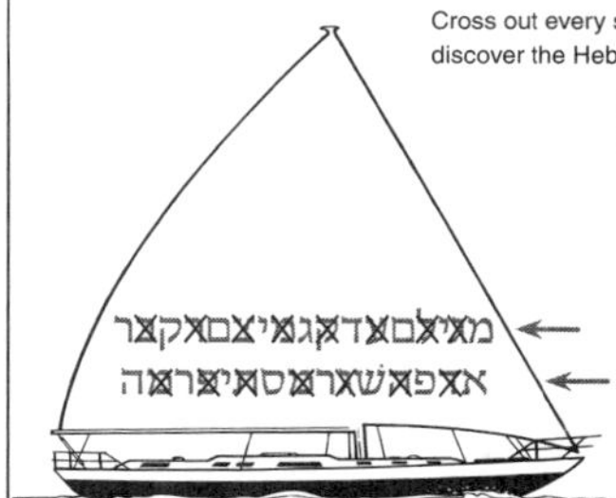

Write the Hebrew words from the boat in the correct spaces.

1. cold ___קַר___
2. boat ___סִירָה___
3. water ___מַיִם___
4. fish (pl) ___דָגִים___
5. it is possible ___אֶפְשָׁר___

80

You're the Author

Complete the sentences using the words below. Read your sentences to a classmate.

דָגִים גָדוֹל אֶפְשָׁר לָבָן קַר

1. אֲנִי רוֹאָה גָמָל ___גָדוֹל___.
2. יֵשׁ הַרְבֵּה ___דָגִים___ בַּיָם.
3. דֶגֶל יִשְׂרָאֵל בְּצֶבַע כָּחוֹל ___וְלָבָן___.
4. חַם בַּמִדְבָּר, ___קַר___ בַּמַיִם.
5. יֵשׁ לִי בֶּגֶד-יָם. ___אֶפְשָׁר___ לָלֶכֶת לַיָם?

דָג בְּצֶבַע כָּחוֹל וְצָהוֹב.

81

Search and Circle

Circle the English meaning for each Hebrew word.

(Monday)	Tuesday	Thursday	1. יוֹם שֵׁנִי
trip	it is possible	(here)	2. פֹּה
water	(salt)	sea	3. מֶלַח
(to go up)	to sing	to sit	4. לַעֲלוֹת
antiquities	(ancient)	more	5. עַתִּיק
ancient	(antiquities)	more	5. עַתִּיקוֹת

Climb Masada

Climb Masada in just five steps. Start at the bottom row and trace a shortcut by finding the Hebrew for the five English words below. Move up one space at a time.

antiquities salt more to go up here

A Perfect Fit

Circle the correct form of the verb in each sentence.

1. אִמָּא אוֹהֵב/(אוֹהֶבֶת) לָלֶכֶת לַיָּם.
2. דָנִיאֵל (רוֹצֶה)/רוֹצָה/רוֹצִים לַעֲלוֹת עַל הָהָר.
3. בֵּן וּמַיָה שָׁר/שָׁרָה/(שָׁרִים) תְּפִילָה.
4. בֵּן (צָרִיךְ)/צְרִיכָה לֶאֱכוֹל.
5. אַתֶּם גָר/גָרָה/(גָרִים) בְּתֵל-אָבִיב.

Put It in Order

Read the sentences below and number them from 1 to 5 in the order that they occur in the story on pages 82-83.

pages 82-83

2 דִינָה: אֶפְשָׁר לְשַׂחֵק בְּיַם-הַמֶּלַח?
3 דָנִיאֵל: אֶפְשָׁר לַעֲלוֹת עַל הָהָר?
1 אִמָּא: בַּמִדְבָּר יֵשׁ עוֹד יָם, יַם-הַמֶּלַח.
4 אַבָּא: עַכְשָׁו אֲנַחְנוּ עַל הָהָר.
5 דִינָה: זֶה מָקוֹם יָפֶה.

CHAPTER

14

Crossword Puzzle

Write the Hebrew translation for each English word in the correct spaces in the crossword.

ACROSS:
1. to put
2. to play
3. to drink
4. to go, to walk
5. to go up

DOWN:
1. to buy
3. to eat
4. to sit
5. to travel
6. to sing

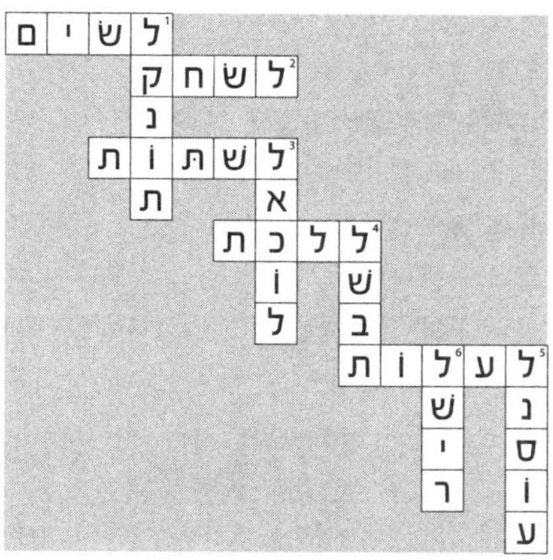

כֵּיף לְשַׂחֵק בַּבּוֹץ בְּיַם הַמֶּלַח.

Make the Connection

Use one of the following words to complete each sentence. Then match the drawings to the sentences.

עַל   עַל-יַד   בַּ___

1. קוֹלָה <u>עַל-יַד</u> מַיִם.
2. מִשְׁפָּחָה <u>בַּ</u>מוֹנִית.
3. כַּדּוּר <u>עַל-יַד</u> תִּיק.
4. כּוֹבַע <u>עַל</u> הָרֹאשׁ שֶׁל דִינָה.

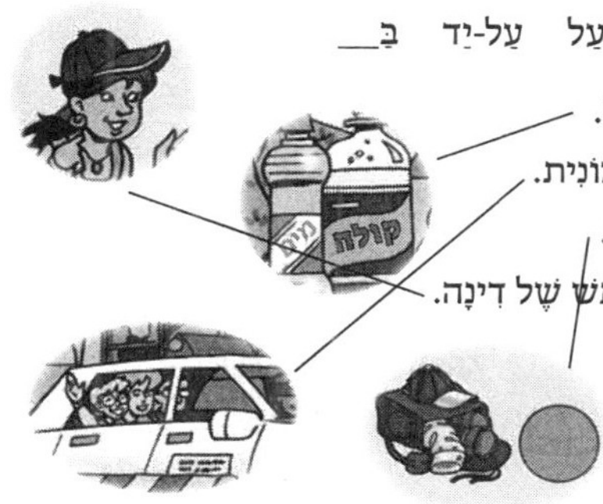

What's the Question?

Use the following words or phrases to answer the questions below.

בַּמִסְעָדָה   בְּיַם-הַמֶּלַח

בַּמִדְבָּר, עַל הַר גָדוֹל   בַּמִדְבָּר

1. אֵיפֹה רוֹצִים לֶאֱכוֹל וְלִשְׁתּוֹת? <u>בַּמִסְעָדָה</u>
2. אֵיפֹה אֶפְשָׁר לָצוּף (to float)? <u>בְּיַם-הַמֶּלַח</u>
3. אֵיפֹה יַם-הַמֶּלַח? <u>בַּמִדְבָּר</u>
4. אֵיפֹה מְצָדָה? <u>בַּמִדְבָּר, עַל הַר גָדוֹל</u>

Watch the Endings

In Hebrew, plural words can end in either ים or ות.

Write each word below in the correct column (one word per row).
Then write its meaning or draw a picture to illustrate it (your choice)!

אֲנָשִׁים מַתָּנוֹת דָּגִים גְּמַלִּים עוּגוֹת כִּפּוֹת

meaning	ות	ים
people		אֲנָשִׁים
gifts	מַתָּנוֹת	
fish (pl)		דָּגִים
camels		גְּמַלִּים
cakes	עוּגוֹת	
skullcaps	כִּפּוֹת	

בַּשּׁוּק אֶפְשָׁר לִקְנוֹת יְרָקוֹת (vegetables).

90

Yes or No?

Read each of the following sentences and based on the story decide whether it is true or false. Circle the letter in the correct column, כֵּן or לֹא.

כֵּן	לֹא	
(ל)	ח	1. בִּבְאֵר-שֶׁבַע אֶפְשָׁר לִקְנוֹת מַתָּנוֹת בַּשּׁוּק.
מ	(ה)	2. אֵין אוּנִיבֶרְסִיטָה בִּבְאֵר-שֶׁבַע.
(ת)	ט	3. יֵשׁ הַרְבֵּה גְּמַלִּים.
ק	(ר)	4. אִמָּא לֹא קוֹנָה מַתָּנוֹת.
צ	(א)	5. מַיָה וְדִינָה נוֹסְעוֹת לְחֵיפָה.
(ו)	ע	6. אַבָּא, אִמָּא וּמַיָה נוֹסְעִים לְנְיוּ-יוֹרְק.
(ת)	נ	7. כֵּיף בְּיִשְׂרָאֵל.

Copy each circled letter in the numbered space below to find a mystery phrase.

שָׁלוֹם חֲבֵרִים, לְהִתְרָאוֹת.

7 6 5 4 3 2 1

91

CHAPTER 15

What's the Question?

Turn each answer below into a question.
Begin with one of the following words:

מִי? אֵיפֹה? מָה?

1. דָּנִיאֵל רוֹאֶה גָּמָל.
   מִי רוֹאֶה גָּמָל? or מָה דָּנִיאֵל רוֹאֶה?
2. אִמָּא וְסַבְתָּא בְּבֵית-הַכְּנֶסֶת.
   מִי בְּבֵית-הַכְּנֶסֶת? or אֵיפֹה אִמָּא וְסַבְתָּא?
3. הַמַּתָּנוֹת בַּתִּיק.
   מָה בַּתִּיק? or אֵיפֹה הַמַּתָּנוֹת?
4. דִּינָה קוֹנָה כּוֹבַע בַּחֲנוּת.
   מִי קוֹנָה כּוֹבַע בַּחֲנוּת? or מָה דִּינָה קוֹנָה בַּחֲנוּת?
5. הַכֹּתֶל בִּירוּשָׁלַיִם.
   אֵיפֹה הַכֹּתֶל? or מָה בִּירוּשָׁלַיִם?

Challenge: Can you think of more than one question for each answer?

Whose Is It?

Choose from the words below to complete each sentence.

שֶׁלִּי שֶׁלְּךָ שֶׁלָּךְ שֶׁלָּנוּ

1. יֵשׁ לִי טַלִּית בְּצֶבַע כָּחוֹל. הַטַּלִּית שֶׁלִּי.
2. הִנֵּה הַדֶּגֶל שֶׁל בֶּן. בֶּן, הַדֶּגֶל שֶׁלְּךָ.
3. אַבָּא וְדָנִיאֵל: הַכִּפּוֹת לֹא שֶׁל סַבָּא וְדוֹד, הַכִּפּוֹת שֶׁלָּנוּ.
4. אֲנַחְנוּ גָּרִים פֹּה. הַבַּיִת שֶׁלָּנוּ.
5. מַיָה, הִנֵּה הַסִּירָה שֶׁלָּךְ.

92

Which Doesn't Belong?

One word in each line doesn't belong. Circle it. Then explain why the word does not fit.

This word doesn't belong because:	
it is not a place	1. עִיר קִבּוּץ הַר (לְשַׂחֵק)
it is not a group of people	2. אֲנָשִׁים (יוֹפִי) יְלָדִים חֲבֵרִים
it is not about families	3. (כַּדּוּרֶגֶל) מִשְׁפָּחָה בֶּן-דוֹד סַבְתָּא
it is not a number	4. עֶשֶׂר שֶׁבַע אֶפֶס (מַתָּנָה)
it is not a drink	5. חָלָב מִיץ (שׁוּק) קָפֶה
it is not a color	6. יָרוֹק (שִׁירִים) צָהוֹב אָדוֹם

Art Critic

In Hebrew, describe the picture below to a classmate.

93